punched

Techniques and Projects for Modern Punch Needle Art

STACIE SCHAAT

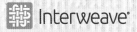

penguinrandomhouse.com

Interweave®

1 3 5 7 9 10 8 6 4 2

SRN: 19SF02

ISBN 13: 978-1-63250-683-2

editorial director: Kerry Bogert

editor: Jodi Butler

editorial coordinator: Hayley DeBerard

technical editor: Debra Fehr Greenway

art director: Ashlee Wadeson

cover & interior designer: Ashlee Wadeson

photographer: George Boe

contents

introduction

I often think back to a surprisingly self-assuring conversation I had several years ago. I was organizing my sewing supplies when my daughter Lenna, who was three years old at the time, came in and asked me what I was up to. I explained to her that I was just cleaning up my craft space. Her eyes widened, her jaw fell dramatically, and she exclaimed, "Mom! You are not a crap face!"

So what do you need to know about me? Well, for starters, I'm not a crap face. Or so I'm told. Some days are better than others.

I do, however, treasure my craft space. I find that I am a better wife, mother, and generally a better human being, when I make time to create. It's my version of self-care, and I honestly don't know who I would be if it weren't for the countless hours that I have spent over the years exploring various creative avenues. While I do have interest in most art forms, time and time again, I find myself drawn to fiber art.

My personal fiber art timeline began almost twenty years ago when I was introduced to sewing. After years of exclusively working with a sewing machine, I eventually tried my hand at weaving, and failed miserably in teaching myself to knit. I'm sure I'll try again eventually—it's what I do!

A few years ago I experienced some creative burnout, and took what I thought was a much needed break from creative work. My husband, Rauland, noticed the void that was left when I stopped creating. That year he gave me a birthday gift that would send me down a creative path I had never imagined for myself. He gave me three different types of rug hooks, explaining that he didn't really understand what they did, but he hoped I would enjoy experimenting with them.

First, I tried locker hooking; then I taught myself to use a traditional rug hook. Not long after, I discovered the punch needle, and I couldn't put it down (I would like to point out how much self-restraint it took not to write "I was hooked" just now. I deserve credit for that).

My goal with *Punched* is to teach you the technical aspects of using a punch needle, so you can get the hang of it just well enough to throw my advice out the window and break into your own creative rhythm.

These tools, methods, and designs are what work well for me. If nothing else, they should prove to be a pretty good launching point for you and your own creative punching journey. And when it's all said and done, I hope you enjoy learning this skill and always remember that you are not a crap face!

Happy Punching,

Stacie

@yellowspool

PUNCH NEEDLE 101

Before the punch needle, there was the traditional rug hook. It resembles a crochet hook, and is used from the front of a fabric canvas to pull loops of yarn up through to the surface of the fabric [**Figure 1**]. It's a two-handed process that is slow and methodical. Sometimes a slow workflow is exactly what the soul needs.

But for those of us who value efficiency, the punch needle is a magnificent tool. With a punch needle, you punch from the back side of the fabric to push yarn through to the front. As you bring the needle back up, the yarn folds in half to create a loop [**Figure 2**]. The repeated punching creates a continuous loop stitch that mirrors the look of a traditional rug hook from the front side.

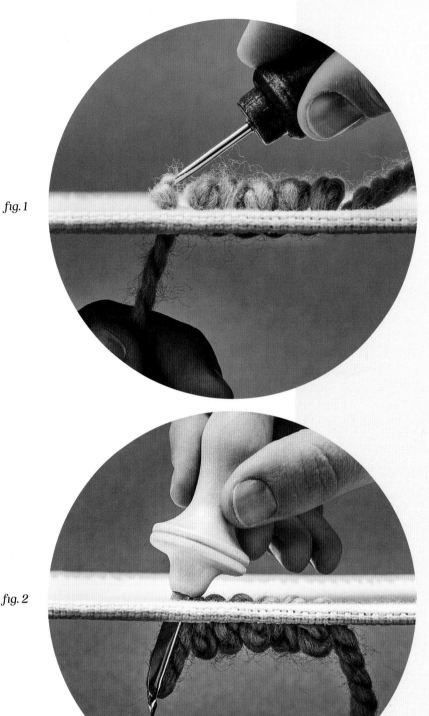

fig. 1

fig. 2

Parts of a Punch Needle

1. **Needle:** The metal tip has a needle's eye for threading with yarn. The height of the needle determines the height of the loops that will be made with the punch needle.

2. **Channel:** A slot running the length of the tool to feed yarn from the skein to the needle tip.

3. **Handle:** Held for control and overall use of the punch needle.

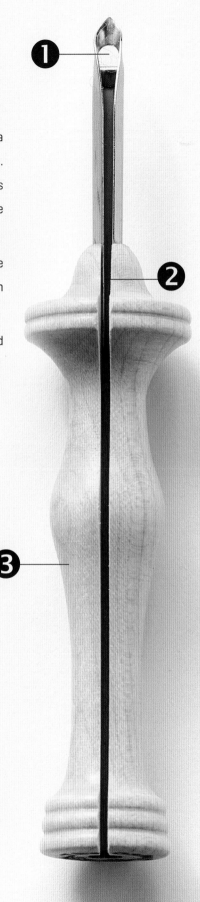

tools & materials

From the moment I started sharing my punch needle work online, I have been flooded with emails asking me what materials are needed to get started. It is challenging to provide an in-depth answer. So I am thrilled to have the space here to categorize the necessary materials, the options within each category, and how to determine which materials are right for you.

TOOLS & SUPPLIES

There are a wide variety of materials that can be used for punching. The following is a list of my beginner-friendly favorites.

Essential Items

Punch needle

Frame

Foundation cloth

Yarn

Scissors

Good-To-Have Items

Tapestry needle

Super glue

Marker, permanent or water-based

Traditional rug hook

Sewing machine

PUNCH NEEDLES

For obvious reasons, this is the most important supply for punching. The punch needle has a needle-like tip, with a hollow handle that allows the yarn to smoothly move through the center of the tool as you work. Some punch needles are adjustable to allow for different loop heights, while others have a fixed height. For the techniques and projects in this book, you will need a punch needle intended for rug hooking, not embroidery.

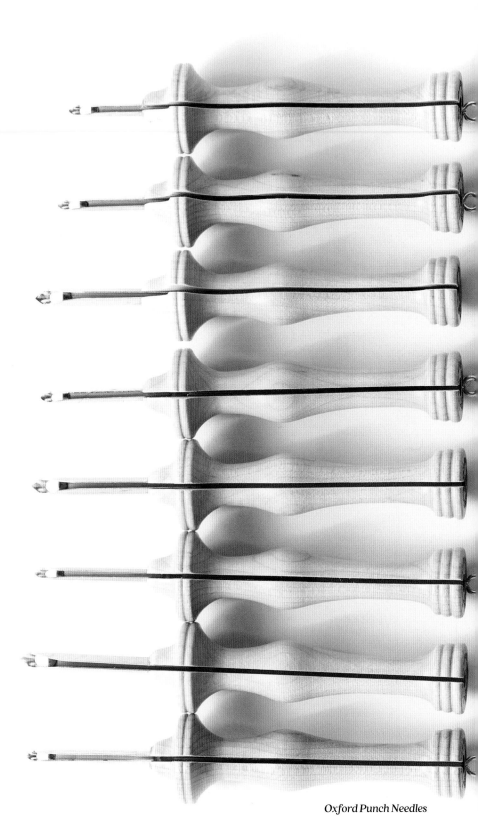

Oxford Punch Needles

Oxford Punch Needle

This high-quality tool is my go-to punch needle because of its reliability and strength. It has a fixed height, with a sturdy wooden handle. The Oxford Company provides eight different punch needles that are sold individually or together in a set. Each punch needle is marked with a sizing number: the larger the number, the shorter the loop it will make.

For beginners, I strongly recommend the size 10 regular—it creates a medium loop height of ¼" (6 mm) with medium weight yarn. The size 14 fine, which creates a shorter loop height of ⅛" (3 mm) with lightweight yarn, is my other favorite. The Oxford punch needle is the one tool that I encourage you to invest in.

NOTE: *Because of my strong preference for this tool, I used two different Oxford punch needles throughout this book, a size 10 regular and a size 14 fine (**Figure 1**).*

Adjustable Punch Needle

An adjustable punch needle gives you the ability to change the height of the loop. (For the one shown here, the "A" setting makes the longest loops.) The adjustable feature lets you achieve varied textures without a full set of punch needles, at a lower price point. There are a lot of different brands that carry adjustable needles. If you decide to buy one, be sure to get a punch needle intended for rug hooking.

The SKC adjustable punch needle shown here (**Figure 2**) is affordable and fairly reliable, but more challenging to thread than the Oxford Punch Needle.

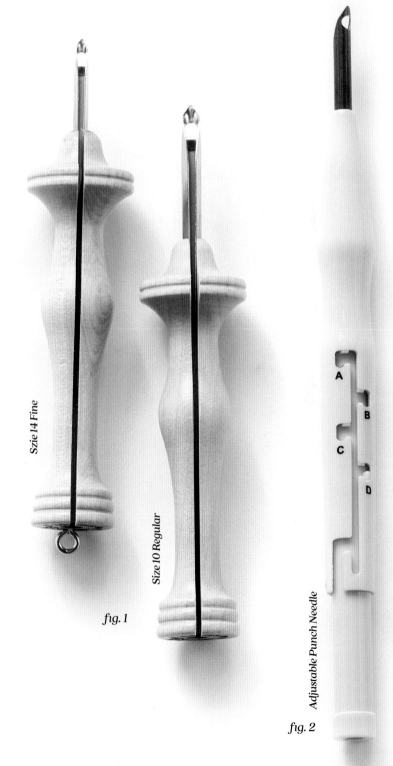

Szie 14 Fine

Size 10 Regular

Adjustable Punch Needle

A
B
C
D

fig. 1

fig. 2

Tip:

Amy Oxford, the maker of the Oxford Punch Needle, provides useful tips and advice about the Oxford Punch Needle on her website: amyoxford.com

Morgan No-Slip Hoop

Hoop Frame

Stretcher Bar Frame

Gripper Frame

FRAMES

To use the punch needle properly, you must attach the foundation cloth (backing material) tightly to a frame to provide stability and tension. A variety of frames were used for the projects in this book. Read about each type to determine which frame will best suit your needs.

Stretcher Bar Frame

Stretcher bars are inexpensive wooden slats that can be easily assembled into a reusable canvas frame. Since you assemble the frame yourself, the size is completely customizable. Stretcher bars work well for making large projects because you can move the project on the frame as you go, meaning you can make a large project on a medium size stretcher bar frame.

Gripper Frame

A gripper frame is more of a financial investment, but it is quicker to set up and grips the foundation cloth securely, making it easy to punch with. Like the stretcher bar frame, the gripper frame is reusable and can be used to make a project larger than the frame itself.

Morgan No-Slip Hoop

Hoops are a less expensive, but more fickle option. The Morgan No-Slip Hoop is the best hoop I've found for keeping the foundation cloth in place as you work. Unlike a standard wooden embroidery hoop, the Morgan No-Slip Hoop is made of plastic and has a subtle groove at the inner hoop, which helps prevent the hoop, and the fabric secured to it, from slipping. This hoop is only suitable for projects that will be smaller than the hoop itself when finished.

Hoop Frame

Another option is to use a standard wooden embroidery hoop, gluing the foundation cloth in place. (Instructions on how to do this can be found in chapter 2.) Because the frame itself is a permanent part of the finished piece, this frame should only be used for projects that will be displayed in the hoop frame.

FOUNDATION CLOTH

You can use any loosely woven, nonstretch fabric to back your project, including linen, twill, and wool felt. There is a lot of room for exploration, but the following types of fabric work wonderfully for beginners.

Monk's Cloth

Monk's cloth is a medium-weight woven cotton fabric. The weave is loose enough that you can see little holes throughout the fabric, but tight enough to hold the yarn securely as you punch.

Not all monk's cloth is created equal, however. In fact, the kind avilable at my local fabric store when I was first getting started was terrible for punching because it was bulky and difficult to maneuver the punch needle into. Purchasing monk's cloth made specifically for rug hooking is an easy way to ensure the fabric will work with a punch needle. The fibers are strong, the weave is even, and it is marked with 2" (5 cm) lines that will help you align and measure your design.

NOTE: *In addition to selling punch needles, The Oxford Company offers a lovely monk's cloth that's marketed for rug hooking and punching. It can also be purchased online through several other rug hooking sites.*

Burlap

Affordable and easily accessible, burlap has been used to hook rugs for ages. When I was new to punching, I used burlap exclusively because it was budget-friendly and suited my needs at the time. Although it's easy to work with, burlap doesn't last as long as monk's cloth because the fibers will disintegrate over time. You can get many years of good use out of burlap, but it's not the best choice if you are hoping to make an heirloom rug that will last for generations. Still, it is a lovely and affordable option for throw pillows and wall hangings.

Other Foundation Cloth Options

Although I usually prefer to go with monk's cloth or burlap, there are many other wonderful fabric choices for punching. Anything with a relatively loose weave and strong fiber, such as linen, wool, or even felt, can be used as a foundation cloth.

Tip:

Bring your punch needle with you when shopping for an alternative foundation cloth, so you can determine how easily your tool will penetrate the material.

Wool

Felt

Monk's Cloth

Linen

Burlap

YARN

I use the term *yarn* loosely here, as you can use yarn, cotton string, fabric scraps, ribbon, and even leather cord with a punch needle. Like every other supply listed, it depends on your personal preference and what you are making. The beauty of punch needle art is that it is so versatile, and using different materials can offer incredible texture and intrigue to a piece.

The yarn weight can be determined by threading the punch needle (see chapter 2) with the desired yarn (or material) and determining how easily it can glide through the punch needle. If the yarn is too thick to pull through the punch needle, it won't work. If the yarn is too thin, it can be folded in half so it is doubled or even tripled in weight when threaded into the punch needle. Be sure to test the yarn weight to make sure it works well with the tool.

Rug Yarn

Sure, rug yarn can be a little pricey, but this wool yarn is made to be walked on, and as such, it stands the test of time. I used yarn from the Seal Harbor Rug Company for several projects in this book. They have over 200 color options to choose from, and their yarn is made to fit a regular-sized punch needle perfectly.

Varied Yarns

Punching is a great way to finish off remnant yarn from other projects. Anything that will glide nicely through the punch needle will work. Using a variety of yarns on one project can create a gorgeous texture variance. The weight of the yarn doesn't need to be precise to fit in a punch needle. As long as it can glide smoothly through the punch needle when threaded, it can be used to punch with.

Tip:

Yarn experimentation adds wonderful texture and interest to your work, but keep in mind that some materials hold up better than others, especially with projects that will get heavier use. For example, fibers such as leather and ribbon will work better for a decorative piece than a rug.

Fabric Scraps

Whether it's quilting cotton or wool strips, fabric of most kinds can be used for punching. Typically, the fabric should be cut into ¼"-wide (6 mm) strips. But this may vary slightly depending on the weight of the fabric. To test your fabric, cut a single ¼"-wide (6 mm) strip, and thread it into the punch needle to determine if that width works before cutting the remainder of the fabric.

Alternative Yarn Options

What else can you use with your punch needle? I've had lovely results with ribbon, leather, metallic cord, and twine. Experiment a little!

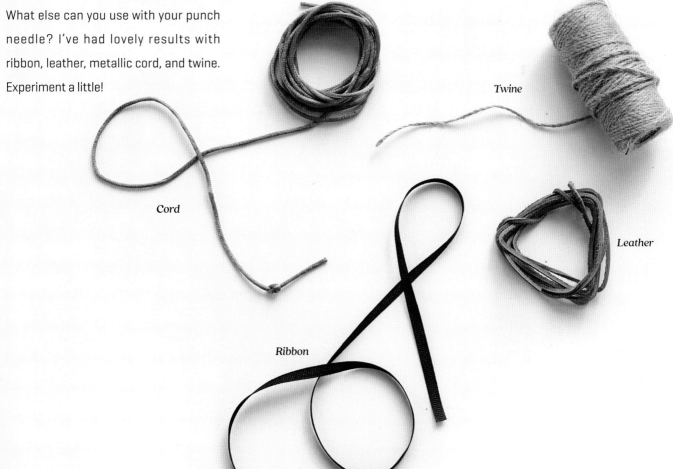

Cord

Twine

Leather

Ribbon

getting started

To enjoy the freedom of the punch needle and all of its possibilities, it is important to understand the basics about punching and how it is done. There is a bit of setup and a few universal rules that you should know before jumping into the various techniques a punch needle can be used for.

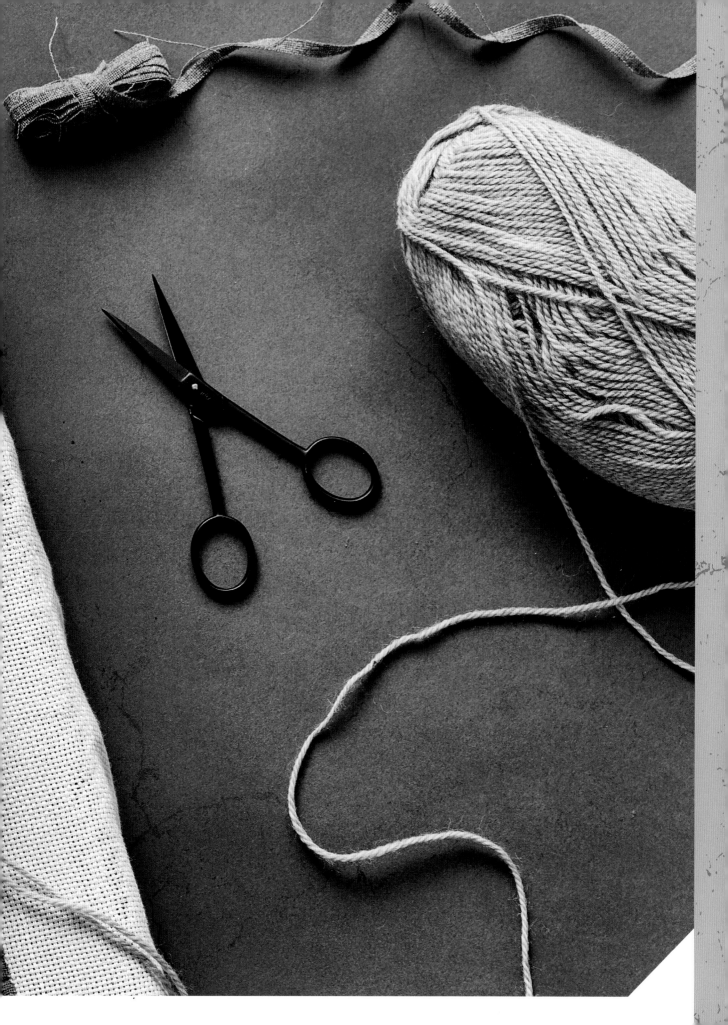

PREPARING THE FOUNDATION CLOTH

I usually draw designs onto fabric freehand, keeping a ruler nearby for straight lines. The beautiful thing about punching: if you don't like the way a drawn design turns out, you can adjust it as you punch. Every drawn line will be covered in the end, so the imperfect patterning on the foundation cloth won't be seen.

Creating the Design

Start by drawing your design on the foundation cloth with a permanent or water-based marker [**Figure 1**]. The punch needle works from the back side of the fabric, so draw the design on the back as a mirror image of what you want the finished piece to look like. This is especially important if the design includes lettering.

Tips:

• Use the grain of the foundation cloth to create straight lines. When outlining a design and drawing straight lines, place the tip of the marker in one of the grooves of the fabric weave and move the marker along the line [**Figure 2**].

• Count squares. For geometric designs involving angled lines, counting the squares in the weave of the foundation cloth can be a great way to help ensure straight lines with even stitches. One way to determine how many squares to count is to find the right angle: place a ruler on the foundation cloth and count how many squares up and over you need to move to maintain that angle. For example, if the foundation cloth has an even weave, counting up two, over two will make a 45-degree angle, while counting up three, over one will make a much steeper angle. Mark these dots [**Figure 3**], and either use them as a guide for your stitches later or use a ruler to draw a solid line connecting the dots.

• Create templates. For a simple, visual layout, creating templates from cardboard or template plastic can be a useful way to orient the design and trace it onto the foundation cloth [**Figure 4**]. This works best with nonlinear or repetitive designs.

• If you find freehand design transfer overwhelming, trace the design from a piece of paper onto the foundation cloth, using a light table or the light from a window. Simply hold the drawing against a sunny window with the cloth on top and trace the design. You can use tape to secure the pieces in place.

fig. 1

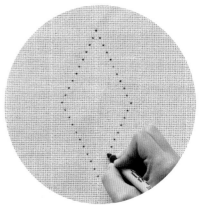

fig. 2

fig. 3

fig. 4

Labeling Patterns

Busy patterns can be confusing to punch. To help keep track of the pattern and which color goes where, you can mark inside the shapes with the first letter of the color or a simple shape that will serve as a reminder along the way [**Figure 1**].

Add a Seam Allowance

Depending on the project, it can be helpful to draw a seam allowance [**Figure 2**]. Whether you are sewing or gluing your punched piece, you will need to cut away excess fabric toward the end of each project. Drawing a seam allowance beforehand makes that step easier.

Securing the Edges

Be sure to leave at least 5" [12.5 cm] of material on all sides of the design. This will help ensure you have enough yardage to secure the foundation cloth to a frame, prevent the cloth from fraying too close to your design, and finish the piece.

To help prevent the foundation cloth from fraying, sew a zigzag stitch around the outer edge before you begin punching [**Figure 3**]. Other methods to secure the edges and prevent fraying:

- Fold under the edge around all sides and secure it in place with double-sided tape to create a hem

- Fold painter's tape around the edges

- Treat the edges with fray glue

- Serge the edges

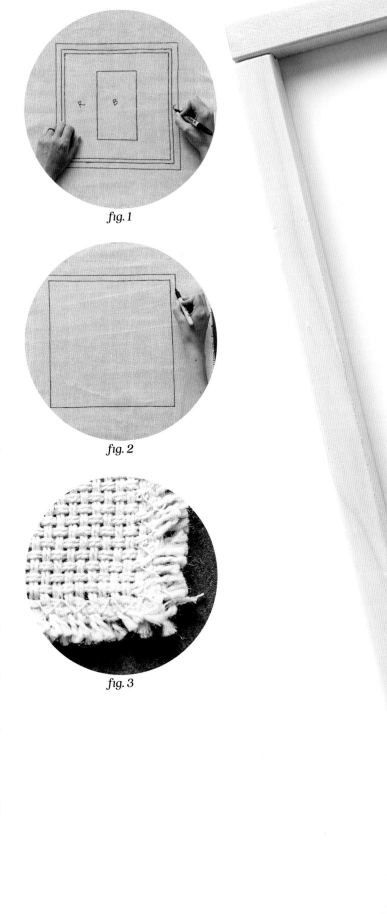

fig. 1

fig. 2

fig. 3

PREPARING THE FRAME

Follow the steps for the type of frame you are using.

Stretcher Bar Frame

To secure the foundation cloth onto a stretcher bar frame, fold under the edge of the cloth about 1" (2.5 cm) on all sides. Using a staple gun or push pins, tack down the folded edge along one side of the frame (**Figure 1**). Pull the cloth tight to tack it onto the remaining sides of the frame in the same manner (**Figure 2**). Tack the corners into the inner edge of the frame as shown (**Figure 3**). When finished, the foundation cloth should be taut and even on the frame (**Figure 4**).

NOTE: *For projects larger than the stretcher bar frame, tack the cloth down with push pins and punch as much as possible within the frame, then remove the push pins. Re-center the foundation cloth to frame the next segment of the piece, and secure it tightly again around all sides with the push pins.*

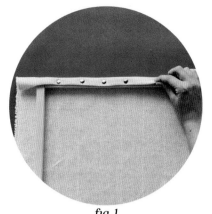

fig. 1

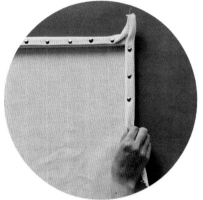

fig. 2

fig. 3

fig. 4

Tip:

A lot of artists use a staple gun to secure their fabric to the frame. I prefer push pins because they are easier to remove afterwards, but you need to keep an eye on them to make sure they don't come loose and get lost.

Gripper Frame

To secure foundation cloth onto a gripper frame, press the foundation cloth into the gripper strip along one side (**Figure 1**). Tug along the remaining three sides, pressing them carefully onto the gripper frame as well. Lift and adjust the foundation cloth on the frame as needed, until it is as taut and even as possible (**Figure 2**). Place the cover around the frame to protect your hands from the gripper strips as you work (**Figure 3**).

NOTE: For projects larger than the gripper frame, first punch as much as possible within the frame. When it is time to move the work, gently remove each side slowly, rolling the cloth off of the gripper strips to avoid snagging any fibers. Re-center the work onto the gripper frame and press it gently in place again, starting with the sides that have already been punched. *The last sides you attach to the frame should be unpunched to make it easier to tug and adjust the foundation cloth without pulling out any of the loops you have already punched.*

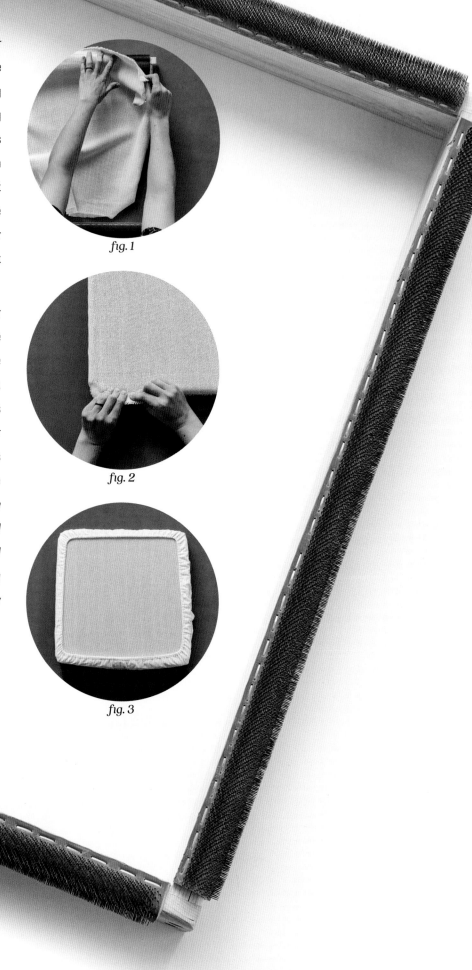

fig. 1

fig. 2

fig. 3

Morgan No-Slip Hoop Frame

The Morgan No-Slip Hoop works wonderfully for projects that are smaller than the frame itself or projects that you plan to remove from the frame when complete. It is not ideal for large projects that will need to be adjusted on the frame as you work.

To secure your foundation cloth onto a Morgan No-Slip Hoop, attach fabric as you would to any embroidery hoop [**Figure 1**]. Tighten the hoop almost all the way, leaving a little bit of wiggle room. Use both hands to pull the fabric taut, as evenly as possible. Tighten the hoop all the way [**Figure 2**].

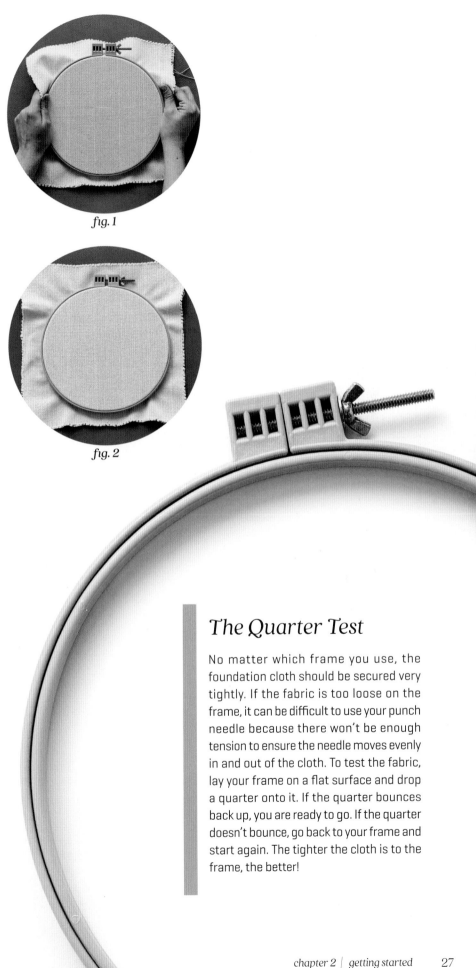

fig. 1

fig. 2

The Quarter Test

No matter which frame you use, the foundation cloth should be secured very tightly. If the fabric is too loose on the frame, it can be difficult to use your punch needle because there won't be enough tension to ensure the needle moves evenly in and out of the cloth. To test the fabric, lay your frame on a flat surface and drop a quarter onto it. If the quarter bounces back up, you are ready to go. If the quarter doesn't bounce, go back to your frame and start again. The tighter the cloth is to the frame, the better!

Hoop Frame

When I first started punching, I noticed several artists using stretcher bar frames to punch their pieces and then transferring the finished design to an embroidery hoop for display. (The foundation cloth tends to loosen in an embroidery hoop as you work.) After seeing a fellow puncher use glue to hold her foundation cloth in place on stretcher bars, I realized I could use a similar technique with a standard embroidery hoop to prevent the foundation cloth from slipping in the hoop.

NOTE: *The following instructions are intended only for projects you plan to both work and display in the embroidery hoop.*

To secure foundation cloth onto a standard embroidery hoop, repeat the process used for the Morgan No-Slip Hoop (**Figure 1**). When the fabric is very taut and the weave seems straight in both directions, cut around the edge, leaving about ½" (1.3 cm) of fabric on all sides (**Figure 2**). Wearing a pair of plastic or rubber gloves, use super glue to secure the raw edges of the fabric to the inner edge of the embroidery hoop. Move slowly around the hoop, only gluing about 2" (5 cm) at a time to ensure the glue holds securely (**Figure 3**). Let the glue dry for a few minutes (**Figure 4**). Once finished, the foundation cloth on the hoop will be secured tightly, ready to display when you are finished punching onto the frame.

fig. 1

fig. 2

fig. 3

fig. 4

USING THE OXFORD PUNCH NEEDLE

Follow these directions to thread and use your punch needle correctly.

NOTE: *These directions show an example of a basic stitch (see chapter 3 for more stitch and technique tutorials).*

Threading the Punch Needle

1. Thread the yarn through the eye of the punch needle (**Figure 1**).

2. Hold the yarn tail securely, then tug on the yarn from the skein to snap the yarn into place inside the channel of the punch needle (**Figure 2**).

3. Test the yarn to make sure it glides smoothly through the needle (**Figure 3**).

NOTE: *If the yarn seems too lightweight for the needle, you can fold it in half to double or even triple it up into the needle to get the weight you want to work with.*

fig. 1

fig. 2

fig. 3

Making the First Punch

1. Thread the needle, leaving a ¼" (6 mm) tail at the tip (**Figure 1**).

2. Working with the channel facing up, punch the needle all the way down into the backing material (**Figure 2**).

3. On the underside of the frame, hold the tail as you pull the punch needle back up (**Figure 3**). This will keep the tail on the front side of your work. You will need the tail to be on the loop side of your work, so you won't have to push the tails through to that side later.

NOTE: *The punch needle creates a continuous loop stitch, meaning that from the back side you can pull the entire stitch out in one simple pulling motion. The front side, with loops, is less likely to pull loose, which is why it's better to keep your tails on the front.*

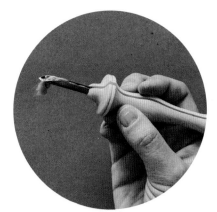

fig. 1

fig. 2

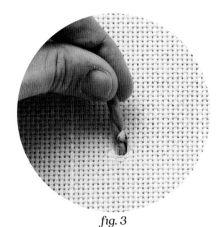

fig. 3

Tips for Success

- To keep the loop heights even, punch the needle all the way down into the fabric (**Figure 1**).

- Lead with the channel. The side of the needle that shows the exposed yarn should be facing in the direction you are punching (**Figure 2**).

- When changing direction, punch the needle all the way down into the fabric before pivoting the punch needle (**Figure 3**).

- Pull the needle up just enough to get the tip of the punch needle back to the surface of the foundation cloth, then glide it about ¼" (6 mm) and punch into the next point. Do not pull the needle too far back up. Doing so will create inconsistent loops and may even undo the most recent punched loop (**Figure 4**).

Changing Colors

To finish punching a color or shape, push the punch needle down into the foundation cloth, then back into the same location of the last stitch to create a backstitch. With the punch needle still pushed down into the foundation cloth, clip the yarn from the loop side (**Figure 5**). (The tail should be on the loop side.) When a piece is completely punched, the tails can be trimmed to the same length as the loops.

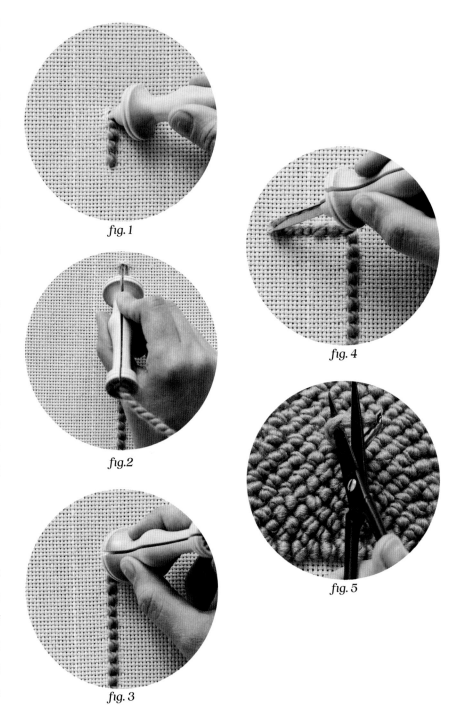

fig. 1

fig.2

fig. 3

fig. 4

fig. 5

Securing Yarn Ends

I am frequently asked why the unknotted tails of yarn don't come undone. Because the tail finishes in such tight quarters the surrounding loops hold it in place. Still, to make sure the yarn tail is secure, I like to make one quick backstitch when I begin a new color. To make a backstitch, begin one stitch ahead of the desired starting point, punch down, pull the tail to the front, punch forward once, and then punch back into the same spot as the first punch (**Figure 1**). This helps hold the tail so it doesn't come loose.

fig. 1

Tip:

Depending on the yarn weight and stitch type, yarn can sometimes start to come undone as you work. To avoid unwanted raveling when this happens, use the tip of one finger to hold the last stitch in place while punching with your other hand (**Figure 2**).

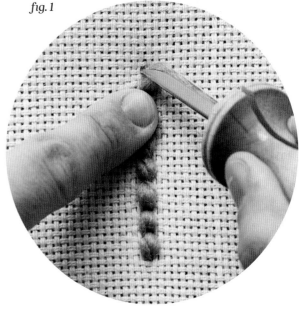

fig. 2

stitches &
technique

One of my favorite things about punching is the abundance of creative freedom. You get to choose your own design and stitches, which materials to use, and how to finish your piece. But in order to make these decisions, it's important to understand the techniques you can use to create your designs. I hope you will feel free to make notes in the margins and bookmark the techniques you plan to return to time and again.

I also want to stress that these are just my favorite techniques. Many are commonly used in the rug hooking and punching communities, while some are methods I came up with to achieve new textures. I encourage you to do the same.

ACHIEVING TEXTURE THROUGH VARIOUS TECHNIQUES

There are many different techniques you can try with a punch needle. Some are traditional, while others are modern approaches that add texture to a piece.

NOTE: *The following stitch guidelines are for an Oxford regular punch needle. When using an Oxford fine punch needle, the standard four stitches per inch (2.5 cm) should be adjusted to six stitches per inch (2.5 cm). If using a fine punch needle, adjust your stitch lengths accordingly.*

Tip

Be careful not to stitch too tightly. Four stitches per inch (2.5 cm) is standard with an Oxford regular-size punch needle. If there are too many loops per inch (2.5 cm), the project will curl in on itself when it is removed from the frame (**Figure 1**). If there are too few loops per inch (2.5 cm), the loops are more likely to come loose with use and look bare on the front side (**Figure 2**). This will quickly become intuitive as you work, but when you are first starting out, it's a good idea to take an occasional peek at the front side of your work as you go to be sure it looks filled in evenly (**Figure 3**).

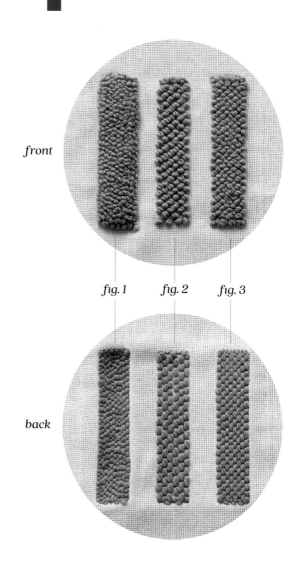

front

fig. 1   fig. 2   fig. 3

back

Basic Stitch

This is the most commonly used stitch type for punching.

Working from the back, punch about four stitches per inch (2.5 cm). Stagger the stitches, like layered bricks, in each row to help space the loops evenly on the front side. The front side is made of loops, while the back side is flat with staggered stitches.

front

back

Outline Stitch

This stitch is commonly used to outline a shape or create a solid line. The stitches are closer together than the basic stitch to avoid gaps in the loops on the front side.

Working from the back, punch about six stitches per inch (2.5 cm). On the front side the loops are close together, creating a solid line for outlining. The back side is flat with short stitch lengths.

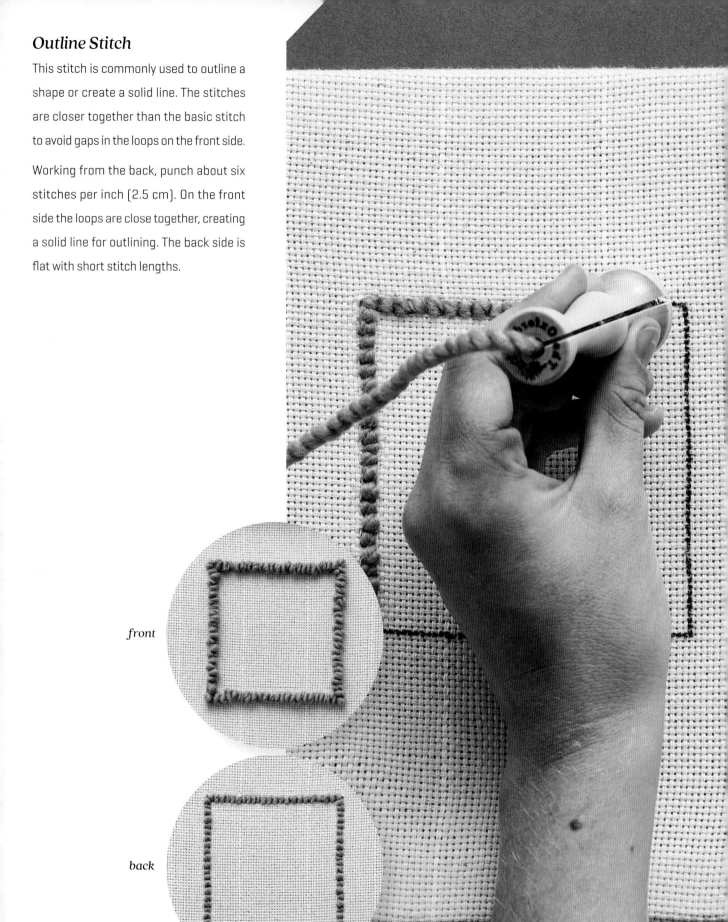

front

back

Dotted Stitch

This stitch has the opposite effect of the outline stitch. The exaggerated length between each stitch staggers the loops on the front side, creating a dotted line.

Working from the back, punch two to three stitches per inch (2.5 cm). Sometimes moving the punch needle this far causes previous stitches to come loose. To avoid this, use your index finger to hold the previous stitch in place as you work. On the front side the loops are distanced, creating a dotted line. The back side is flat with long stitch lengths.

front

back

Ribbed Stitch

The goal of this stitch is to work in rows, lining up each stitch with the previous row. Working in horizontal rows on the back side creates vertical ribbing on the front side, as the loops line up perfectly.

Working from the back, use four stitches per inch (2.5 cm) to create straight lines. Row by row, punch in an identical pattern to the previous row. On the front side, the loops are lined up evenly, creating a ribbed effect. The back is flat, with perfectly even stitches that are lined up row by row.

front

back

Flat Stitch

The flat stitch displays what is typically the back side of a basic stitch.

Working from the front side, stitch about four stitches per inch (2.5 cm), staggering the stitches in each row, like layered bricks. The front side displays the flat stitches, while the back has loops.

front

back

Fringed Loops

This stitch is done in a single row, usually layered over a flat stitch. It is made up of very long stitches that drape like fringe.

Working from the back, push the punch needle all the way into the backing material. From the underside of the working piece (the front), gently pull the yarn through the punch needle to lengthen it several inches. Repeat in a line to create fringed loops. These loops can be left as-is or be trimmed on the front side. The back looks like a single row of basic stitching.

front

back

Heightened Stitch

The heightened stitch is used to create lengthened loops on the front side of your piece. This technique is especially helpful if you don't have an adjustable punch needle but would like longer loops for part or all of the project.

Working from the back, push the punch needle all the way into the backing material. From the underside (the front side) of the piece, gently pull the yarn at different lengths for each stitch. This creates a heightened length on the front, while the back side is flat and looks like the back of a basic stitch.

front

back

Tufted

After punching with a basic stitch, the loops can be trimmed on the right side to create a soft, tufted texture.

Use a basic stitch to fill in the desired area to be tufted, then remove the foundation cloth from the frame. On the front side, trim the loops with a pair of scissors. When trimmed, the front side will resemble velvet. The back is flat and looks like the back of a basic stitch.

front

back

MAKING MISTAKES

One of the best things about the punch needle is how forgiving it can be. If you're not happy with a shape or color, you can simply take it out and start over. Strange as it may sound, a lot of punch needle artists, myself included, find this process of undoing work quite satisfying.

Frogging

To take out your stitches, pinch a strand of yarn from the back (flat) side of your work and pull [**Figure 1**]. Simple as that. Anecdotally, the term *frogging* references a play on words, as "rip-it, rip-it" sounds like a frog's "ribbit, ribbit."

Scratching

After a section of work has been taken out, scratching the foundation cloth can help to restore the weave of the material to the state it was in before frogging. You can do this with your fingernail or with the tip of the punch needle. First scratch vertically, then horizontally [**Figure 2**]. This moves the threads in the cloth's weave back to their original place and helps close up any large holes created by the punch needle and yarn used previously.

Tip

If a portion of your work has been taken out, save your yarn. It can be incorporated into other projects, including the Scrappy Rug project in chapter 6.

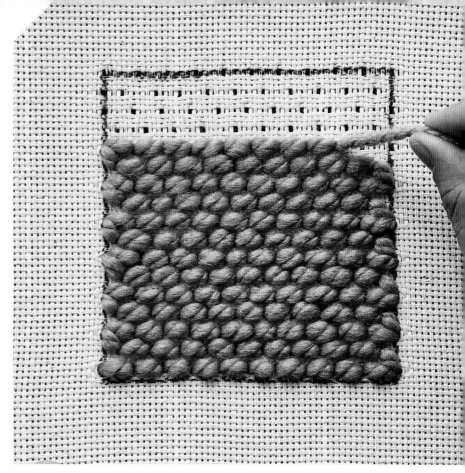

fig. 1

fig. 2

CHAPTER 4

finishing
techniques

Most of the work that goes into a project is done in the punching phase, but sometimes finishing a project can somehow feel more daunting than the rest. Hopefully this next chapter will set your mind at ease. It really is going to be great.

BINDING

Hemmed Edge

The hemmed edge is used to finish a flat piece of work, like a rug or a wall hanging. It folds under several inches of excess foundation cloth, which makes it easy to take apart and fix the rug later if need be.

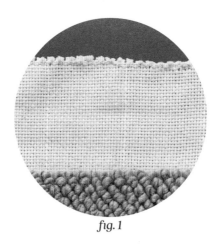

fig. 1

1. Trim the excess fabric, leaving 3" (7.5 cm) around all sides [**Figure 1**]. Sew a zigzag stitch around the edges.

NOTE: For alternative methods for preventing fabric from fraying, see Securing the Edges in chapter 2.

2. With the right side down, press the 3" (7.5 cm) edge under on one side [**Figure 2**].

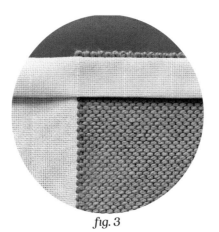

fig. 2

3. Fold the edge in towards the center of the fold, creating a 1½" (3.8 cm) double hem and press flat [**Figure 3**]. Repeat steps 1–3 on all sides.

4. Using a needle and thread, sew a running whipstitch to secure the folded edge of the foundation cloth in place [**Figure 4**].

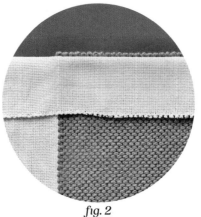

fig. 3

fig. 4

Whipped Edge

A whipped edge is used to bind the finished edge of a flat piece of work, such as a rug or a wall hanging. It can also be used to finish the upper edge of a bag or pocket.

1. Cut the excess fabric around all sides of the piece to about 1" (2.5 cm) and sew a zigzag stitch around the edges (**Figure 1**).

2. Thread a tapestry needle with a double strand of yarn (**Figure 2**).

3. Bring the needle through from the front of the rug, right alongside the punched edge, and pull the yarn almost all the way through (**Figure 3**). Secure the yarn by threading the needle through the loop and pulling tight (**Figure 4**). This locks the first binding stitch in place without the need for a knot!

4. Fold the edge of the foundation cloth towards the front of the piece, about ¼" (6 mm), and then fold again to tuck the zigzagged edge into the binding (**Figure 5**).

5. Use yarn and a tapestry needle to whipstitch along the edges, being sure to fold the edges of the foundation cloth toward the front of the piece as you work (**Figure 6**).

6. To tie off the yarn, thread the needle through about 3" (7.5 cm) of previously bound edge, and cut the thread (**Figure 7**).

fig. 1

fig. 2

fig. 3

fig. 4

fig. 5

fig. 6

fig. 7

GLUE

Some projects, used for display, can be glued to finish. Whether the punched piece is glued to the back of a frame or another object, such as a lamp shade, the general rules are the same.

fig. 1

1. Cut the excess foundation cloth away, leaving a ½" (1.3 cm) allowance for gluing later (**Figure 1**).

2. Optional: Zigzag the raw edges to prevent fraying (**Figure 2**).

NOTE: *For alternative methods of preventing fabric from fraying, see Securing the Edges in chapter 2.*

3. Using super glue, adhere the edge in small increments. Hold the glued section in place until dry before moving on to the next section (**Figure 3**).

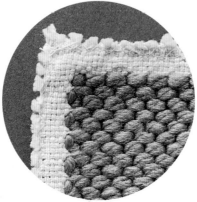

fig. 2

Tip

Wear plastic or rubber gloves to protect your hands from the glue.

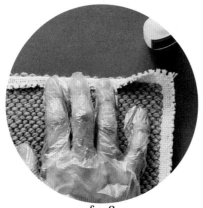

fig. 3

SEW

If a punched piece is going to be turned into a multi-dimensional product, like a bag or a pillow, it can be sewn by hand or sewing machine.

fig. 1

1. When the punched piece is finished, trim the excess foundation cloth, leaving at least ½" (1.3 cm) seam allowance [**Figure 1**].

2. Zigzag the raw edges to prevent raveling [**Figure 2**].

NOTE: *For alternative sewing methods, see Securing the Edges in chapter 2.*

3. Use pins to keep the fabric from sliding as you work, and carefully remove each pin before it reaches the needle as you sew [**Figure 3**].

4. To prevent the loops from getting caught in the needle as you work, push the loops towards the center of the punched piece [**Figure 4**].

fig. 2

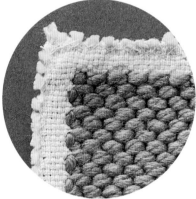

fig. 3

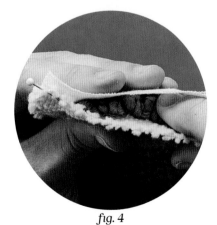

fig. 4

FRINGE

Fringe is tied using the remainder of the backing material to secure the edges of a flat piece of work. It can be used for rugs and wall hangings. If you intend to use a fringe edge for some, but not all sides, finish the fringed sides before the bound edges to prevent accidentally cutting or sewing the cloth threads you will need for tying the fringe.

fig. 1

1. Pull out and set aside the cloth threads running horizontally from the excess foundation cloth along the entire length of the piece. Leave 5 rows of cloth threads running horizontally along the edge of the punched piece (**Figure 1**).

2. Using two separate pieces of the un-tied fringe, tie a simple knot. Continue tying these knots along the length of the piece (**Figure 2**).

NOTE: *For thin fringe, skip to step 6. For fuller fringe, continue to step 3.*

3. Using the discarded foundation cloth threads from step 1, fold each thread in half twice (**Figure 3**).

4. Use a traditional rug hook or a crochet hook to pull the folded loop from step 3 through two of the previously tied knots (**Figure 4**).

5. Pull the thread tails through the loop. and tighten (**Figure 5**). This is called a rya knot. Repeat steps 3–5 along the entire length of the piece.

6. Trim to the desired length (**Figure 6**).

fig. 4

fig. 2

fig. 5

fig. 3

fig. 6

CHAPTER 5

design &
experimentation

This chapter is dedicated to design and exploration. Ultimately, I decided to share my design process, in the hope that you could use it to develop your own. Maybe you already feel comfortable with design and maybe you don't. This is a good place to start.

I hope that as you find your voice and master your own creative process, you will share your process photos on Instagram (#PunchedProject), so I can see your progress and your beautiful creations.

← Heightened
Stitch

← Basic
stitch

← Basic
Stitch

color
gradient

KEEPING A SKETCHBOOK HANDY

I have several sketchbooks at any given time, bursting with potential designs. As hard as I try to keep my ideas organized, these sketchbooks always end up filled with notes about using the design, project types and dimensions, and color concepts.

While these notes may not seem coherent to an onlooker, I use them all the time and they definitely benefit my work. I particularly like having small sketchbooks on hand that fit inside my bag, because you never know when inspiration will strike. And I like being able to jot down an idea wherever I am in the moment.

Sketchbook Organization

Although my sketchbooks don't always stay organized, I still try! I like to make cardstock templates of different shapes (square, rectangle, circle, triangle) to help me quickly outline several shapes at once and brainstorm different ideas within each outline. Sometimes it helps to have side-by-side sketches of different ideas on one page to help figure out which design works the best.

I also try to date my sketches. I don't add the date every time I doodle something new in my sketchbook, but occasionally marking the date allows me to visualize how my inspiration and aesthetic is changing with time. It's helpful and interesting to look back on previous ideas.

Journal Design Inspirations

If a particular design is inspired by something, I always record the source. It is so easy to forget those things. But how priceless to remember that a design was inspired by a quiet moment on the river bank, a recent family visit, or any of the other countless sources of inspiration.

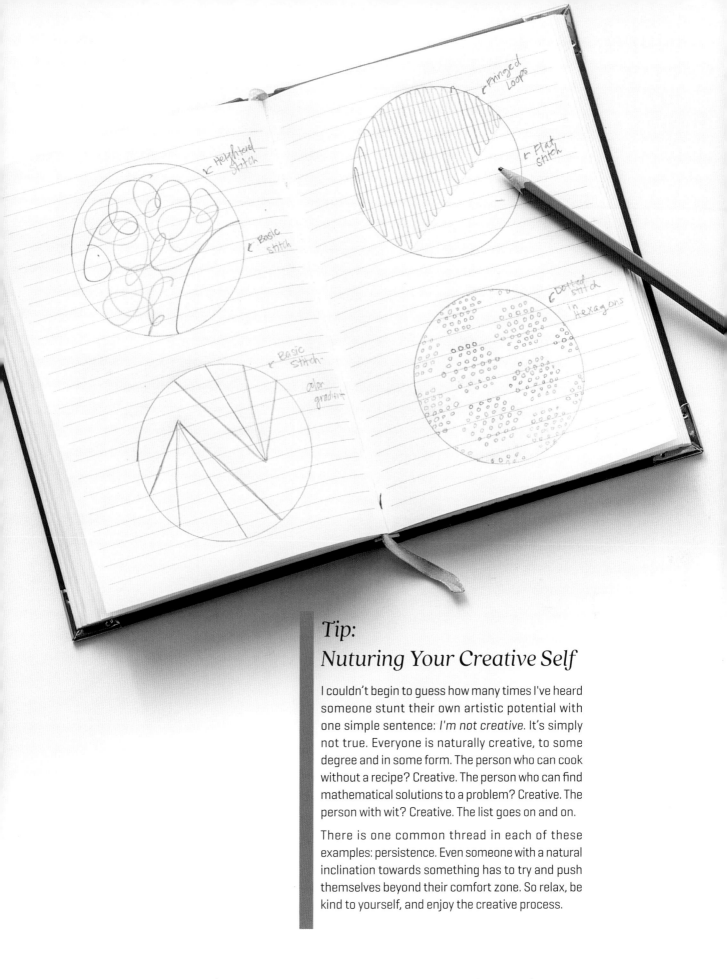

Tip:
Nuturing Your Creative Self

I couldn't begin to guess how many times I've heard someone stunt their own artistic potential with one simple sentence: *I'm not creative*. It's simply not true. Everyone is naturally creative, to some degree and in some form. The person who can cook without a recipe? Creative. The person who can find mathematical solutions to a problem? Creative. The person with wit? Creative. The list goes on and on.

There is one common thread in each of these examples: persistence. Even someone with a natural inclination towards something has to try and push themselves beyond their comfort zone. So relax, be kind to yourself, and enjoy the creative process.

FINDING YOUR STYLE

Honestly, this is a continual journey for me. I've found that locking myself in too tightly to a certain project type or style can lead to creative burnout—fast. There is so much to try, and it is limiting to close the door on design techniques that are less familiar. There is no harm in experimenting.

Linear Design

Linear design can consist of stripes, right angles, and squares. It is simple, relatable to a lot of people, and pairs well with neutral, monochromatic tones, as well as bright and bold color choices.

Linear design is transferred to the foundation cloth by creating marks along the weave of the cloth for straight horizontal and vertical lines. Use a ruler for angled lines.

Repetitive Design

This type of design creates the effect of a kaleidoscope or patterned tile. It is made by outlining a square, triangle, or diamond, and drawing shapes that repeat in the corners and sometimes in the center. When the design is repeated, it creates a larger, more complex visual.

Repetitive design offers endless possibilities and can be scaled to any size. If you use repetitive design for a pillow, say, you might get four pattern repetitions. However, that same design, when used for a rug, might repeat a dozen times or more! It's simply a matter of repeating the design until you get the desired project size.

Plotted Design

This is a common patterning technique that is far less exact than either linear design or repetitive design. A plotted design might consist of curved lines and freehand images. These designs can be traced onto the foundation cloth from a paper pattern, but work very well for freeform drawing, as well.

Whether the pattern is floral, abstract, or anything in between, plotted design is usually asymmetrical, and visually playful.

RUG STUDIES

I took on rug hooking because I wanted to learn to make a rug. My first project was a long runner. Although I was happy with it in the end, it was too ambitious for my first attempt. The project was time consuming and a bit discouraging. In retrospect, I wish I had slowed down to get comfortable with the craft and learn the ins and outs of punching before I attempted a runner.

Since then, I have started making small project samples that I call rug studies. I'm so glad I took the time to experiment on a smaller scale. I'm a bit afraid of color and gravitate toward neutral hues for clothes and decor. I find myself doing the same in my work. Creating small rug studies to test color, pattern, and texture gives me the confidence I need to approach the same decisions and techniques when I'm working on a larger scale project.

Rug studies aren't made to be displayed; they're entirely for experimentation. The goal is to get outside of your comfort zone and try something. There is always something to be learned from trying something new, whether you consider it a poor attempt or a successful one. If you happen to love your rug study, display the finished work in the little hoop frame. For examples, turn the page.

Share Your Work

As you create different rug studies, I hope you will post photos on social media with #RugStudy so your experimentations will appear right alongside my own!

Rug Study Samples

Rug Study #1

A study of texture achieved with stitches and layers, but without color or material variation.

Color: cream, monochrome

Design: simple angled line

Texture: flat stitch, fringed loops, layered

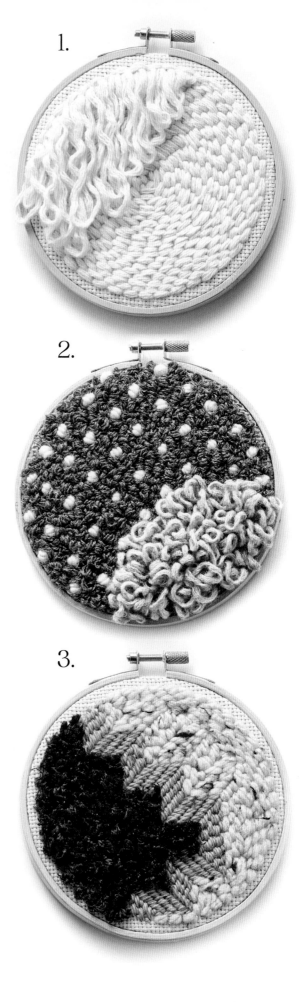

Rug Study #2

A study of the contrast of two different stitch types in a monochromatic color scheme.

Color: cream, light gray, dark gray

Design: curved line, polka dots

Texture: basic stitch (dark gray), dotted stitch (cream), heightened stitch (light gray)

Rug Study #3

A study of color gradient, paired with linear design and textural contrast.

Color: flecked gray, light purple, dark purple, gradient

Design: linear design with right angles

Texture: flat stitch (light purple, flecked gray), tufted (dark purple)

Rug Study #4

A study of the visual and textural effect of using the ribbed stitch in different directions.

Color: peach, brown, pink, yellow

Design: four quadrants of color

Texture: ribbed stitch (rug yarn), altering direction

Rug Study #5

A study of bold color paired with a repetitive pattern.

Color: navy, beige, yellow, pink, maroon, blue, red

Design: repetitive diamonds

Texture: basic stitch (varied yarn)

Rug Study #6

A study of the textural differences between different yarn types: ribbon, twine, metallic cord, fabric, leather-look vinyl.

Color: neutrals

Design: stripes, separating rows of different yarn types

Texture: flat stitch (cream), basic stitch (ribbon, twine, metallic cord, fabric, leather-look vinyl)

4.

5.

6.

the projects

In this chapter, you will find creative designs that incorporate the techniques you have learned so far. You can make them as is or feel free to experiment with the projects to make them your own.

little adventure patches

My husband, Rauland, and I spent the first eight years of our marriage pursuing college degrees and having children. We had big dreams, very little free time, and even less money.

During these years we learned a lot about patience and that we didn't need much to experience adventure together. Some of my fondest memories from those days were when Rauland took time off from school for spontaneous outings and adventures. We played games, developed new skills, and had after-dinner dance parties. For us, these are the moments that add up to a beautiful life and experiences I hope to never forget.

The patches here are meant to celebrate those defining moments in life, whether big or small. It could be a patch to represent a favorite nature escape, a newfound hobby, or a beloved pet. It's your little adventure, so create something that is meaningful to you.

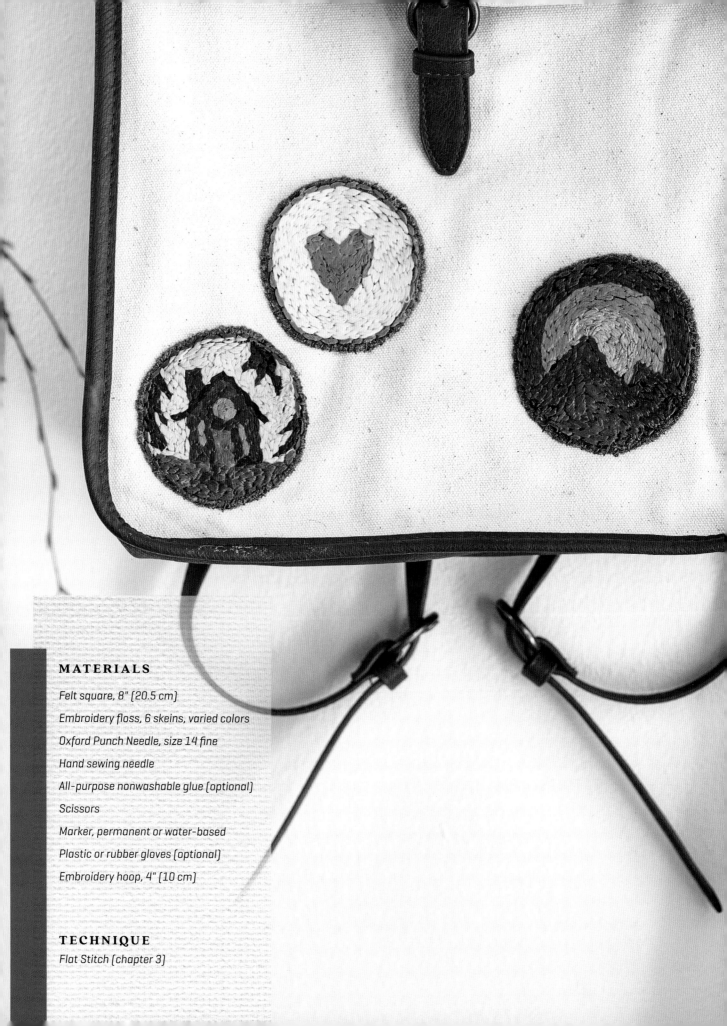

MATERIALS

Felt square, 8" (20.5 cm)

Embroidery floss, 6 skeins, varied colors

Oxford Punch Needle, size 14 fine

Hand sewing needle

All-purpose nonwashable glue (optional)

Scissors

Marker, permanent or water-based

Plastic or rubber gloves (optional)

Embroidery hoop, 4" (10 cm)

TECHNIQUE

Flat Stitch (chapter 3)

fig. 1

fig. 2

fig. 3

fig. 4

fig. 5

fig. 6

1. Trace a small round object, such as a lid or a roll of tape onto the backing cloth, then draw in the design [**Figure 1**].

2. Secure the felt to an embroidery hoop as shown [**Figure 2**].

NOTE: *Don't worry about gluing the hoop or using a Morgan No-Slip Hoop. The felt will naturally stretch a bit and will need to be readjusted onto the embroidery hoop as you work.*

3. Use doubled embroidery floss to punch in the design using a flat stitch [**Figure 3**].

4. Optional: Wearing a pair of plastic or rubber gloves, rub a light layer of the all-purpose nonwashable glue over the surface of the patch [**Figure 4**]. Wait several hours for the glue to dry.

NOTE: *The flat stitch will be the right side [**Figure 5**].*

5. Trim the excess felt, leaving about ¼" [6 mm] seam allowance around all sides [**Figure 6**].

6. Use a simple whip stitch to sew the patch onto a backpack or jacket [see the patches on the opposite page].

belonging pendant

I am the second youngest of five children. All of my siblings have brown hair and beautiful olive skin, like our parents. As a child, I had hair so blonde it was nearly white and the fair skin to go along with it.

One Sunday morning while attending church, a man sitting behind our family tapped my older sister on the shoulder and said, "I see you brought the neighbor girl!" Clearly, he had just noticed the contrast in my hair color. My sisters turned around, not sure if he was serious and told him that I was their sister—the same sister who attended church with them every week.

For whatever reason, this moment of confusion lived on hilariously in our family and I earned the loving nickname of "neighbor girl." I realize a nickname like that has the potential to make a child feel like an outsider, but given the attitude that surrounded it, it made me feel incredibly safe and welcome. Even at a young age, I knew the only reason the nickname stuck was because it was so preposterous that I could belong with anyone else.

Our appearances, backgrounds, stories, and struggles are all unique. And I wanted to create a pendant to symbolize the comfort in finding our place. There is nothing more valuable than the feeling of belonging, and I hope my own children feel as confident in their unconditional place in our family as I do in mine.

MATERIALS

Burlap, 12" (30.5 cm) square

Yarn remnants, 2 colors

Oxford Punch Needle, size 10 regular

Frame pendant (the one shown measures 1½" [3.8 cm]

Super glue

Scissors

Marker, permanent or water-based

Plastic or rubber gloves (optional)

Morgan No-Slip Hoop

TECHNIQUES:

Basic Stitch (chapter 3)

Tufting (chapter 3)

Glue Finish (chapter 4)

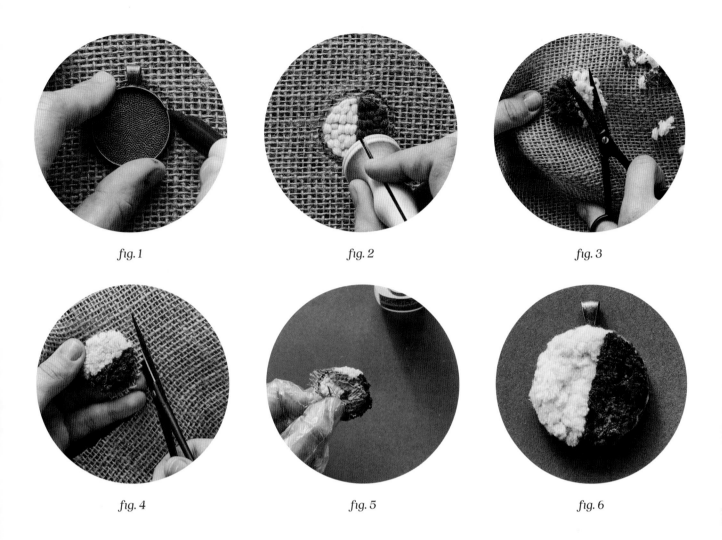

fig. 1   fig. 2   fig. 3

fig. 4   fig. 5   fig. 6

1. Secure burlap in the Morgan No-Slip Hoop and trace the pendant onto the foundation cloth (**Figure 1**).

NOTE: *The actual area you punch will be slightly smaller than the outline.*

2. Draw a line down the center to create separate areas for each of the two yarn colors. Then punch into the foundation cloth as shown (**Figure 2**).

3. Remove the foundation cloth from the hoop and use a pair of sharp scissors to tuft the loops (**Figure 3**).

4. Trim the excess fabric, leaving about ¼" (6 mm) seam allowance around all sides (**Figure 4**).

5. Fold under the excess fabric and glue in place (**Figure 5**).

6. Add glue to the inside of the pendant; then set the punched piece inside the frame. Hold in place until the glue is set, about 60 seconds (**Figure 6**).

Variations:
SO MANY PENDANTS

If you want to try a different type of design, this small-scale tufted project would look wonderful with a simple heart design in the center. Alternatively, sketch out a simple combination of geometric shapes to create your pendant.

Tip:

There are so many ways to display this frame pendant. Slip it onto a keychain, attach it to a zipper, or add a pin to the back and wear it as a brooch.

plant lady basket

I remember the day I brought home my first plant, a cactus. Nothing felt more grown-up at the time than being regimented enough to remember to water a plant. I beamed every time I walked past it. I watered it diligently and found it a happy spot with plenty of sunshine. But it always looked parched. So I started watering it more and more frequently until, before I knew it, I had accidentally drowned it.

The thing is, though, as hard as it may be to properly care for a plant, we still try because the life that a plant breathes into our home is worth the effort. Plants have a way of brightening up a space and giving it that perfect final touch. Although fake plants can do a pretty good job of that, too—and I have yet to kill one of them!

Of course, this basket can be used to house more than plants, and once you've made one, you won't want to stop. If you're anything like me, you'll find endless uses for a pretty basket.

MATERIALS
(FOR ONE BASKET)

Monk's cloth, 24" (61 cm) square

*Cotton fabric, 16" (40.5 cm) circle
(Note: Trace the mouth of your pot to
make a perfect circle and add about 2"
(5 cm) around the edge)*

Cotton string or white yarn, 1 ball or skein

Gold cord, 5 yards (4.6 m)

Matching thread

Oxford Punch Needle, size 10 regular

Tapestry needle

Scissors

Marker, permanent or water-based

*Stretcher bars or gripper frame, 18"
(45.5 cm)*

Sewing machine

*Pot for a plant, about 14" (35.5 cm)
circumference*

TECHNIQUES:

Basic Stitch (chapter 3)

Fringed Loops (chapter 3)

Flat Stitch (chapter 3)

Whipped Edge Finish (chapter 4)

Sewn Finish (chapter 4)

fig. 1

fig. 2

fig. 3

fig. 4

fig. 5

fig. 6

1. Draw a 15" × 6" (38 cm × 15 cm) outline onto the foundation cloth, then mark another outline ½" (1.3 cm) outside of that to account for the seam allowance (**Figure 1**). Secure the foundation cloth to the frame.

NOTE: *The size of the outline may vary depending on the size of your basket. The length of your punched piece should be at least 2" (5 cm) longer than the circumference of the widest part of the planter that will sit inside.*

2. Begin punching the gold stripes on the upper third of the piece using a basic stitch (**Figure 2**).

3. Using the cotton string, punch one row with a basic stitch, and then one row of fringed loops on the lower third of the piece. The fringe should hang most of the way to the bottom of the piece, leaving ½–1" (1.3–2.5 cm) space at the bottom (**Figure 3**).

4. On the right side of the piece, fill in the rest of the space with rows of flat stitches, including the space under the fringed loops (**Figure 4**).

5. Sew a zigzag around all four sides of the piece and trim excess fabric, leaving ½" (1.3 cm) seam allowance (**Figure 5**).

6. With right sides out, create a tube by overlapping the short ends of the piece and whipstitching them together, working from the bottom to the top (**Figure 6**).

7. When you reach the top, continue to whipstitch around the upper edge of the basket to finish the top of the basket [**Figure 7**].

8. Turn the tube inside out. Pin the circular bottom to the lower edge of the punched piece [**Figure 8**]. Sew together on a sewing machine. Trim extra fabric, if needed.

9. Turn the basket right-side out [**Figure 9**] and fill with a plant or anything else!

fig. 7

fig. 8

fig. 9

Variations:
JUST MY SIZE

Want to make a basket in a different size? Follow these instructions for customizing your design.

1. Determine the height and circumference of the basket you want to make. Then use these dimensions to outline the rectangle onto the foundation cloth.

2. To calculate the size of the circular bottom, you will need to find the radius of the circle:

Radius = circumference/6.28

The circumference to use in this equation is the length of the rectangle from step 1.

Then, add ½" (1.3 cm) to the radius, to account for the seam allowance. Draw the circle onto the cotton fabric (a compass works well).

printed burlap wall hanging

My oldest daughter, Lenna, loves insects. Recently, she learned about bug collections and began scheming to gather insects for her own display. Until she realized the insects had to be killed before they could be framed. She couldn't bring herself to capture any insects for that fate, so she opted to search the yard for ones that had already died. With the help of her sister Bev, she had found a beetle and a ladybug to put in a jar. I was impressed that they found anything, but she was discouraged. With the expectations she had set for herself, it was taking longer than she hoped. The next thing I knew, Bev came running inside screaming "Mom! Stop Lenna! She's swatting at a bee, hoping it will sting her!"

Apparently Lenna had determined that if the bee died of natural causes, like after

stinging someone, it fell within her ethical guidelines. I stopped her, of course, and we decided it was time to take a break from the bug collection.

Soon after, I found this butterfly burlap. I knew I had to frame a few butterflies for my little collectors. It was a perfect compromise and allowed them both to help me choose the colors for each butterfly.

The beauty of printed burlap is that you can find it in many different patterns. And because it is framed to hang on the wall, it gets very little wear and tear, making the burlap a perfectly good foundation cloth. It also allows you to punch as loosely as you want, so those printed lines can show between the colors of yarn.

MATERIALS

Printed burlap, any print, 24" (61 cm)

Yarn, varied colors, 2 skeins total

Yarn, background color, 1 skein

Oxford Punch Needle, size 10 regular

Super glue

Scissors

Marker, permanent or water-based

Plastic or rubber gloves (optional)

Stretcher bars or gripper frame, 18" (45.5 cm)

Picture frame, any size

Sewing machine

TECHNIQUES

Flat Stitch (chapter 3)

Glued Finish (chapter 4)

fig. 1

fig. 2

fig. 3

fig. 4

fig. 5

fig. 6

1. Lay the frame on the burlap and find the print arrangement you want to frame. Mark the outline of your piece by tracing the inner edge of the frame or the glass from the frame, if removable (**Figure 1**).

2. Use a flat stitch to loosely fill in the design (**Figure 2**).

NOTE: *Some parts may be really small, like one or two stitches in a certain color. If this* is the case, you can tie a knot on the back side with the yarn tails to secure them. The back won't be seen, so this will not affect the aesthetic (**Figure 3**).

3. With the colorful portions of the design complete, fill in the negative space with the background color (**Figure 4**).

4. Cut the excess fabric away, leaving about 1" (2.5 cm) around all edges. Secure the edges with a zigzag stitch (**Figure 5**).

5. Glue the finished piece to the back of the frame (**Figure 6**).

Variations:
LINES BY DESIGN

Printed burlap can be found in many different patterns. You can also make your own designs. Here are some tips for creating a customized piece:

• Find a frame you love. It can be any shape or size. But a fun frame can really make this project special.

• Select a printed burlap or use a marker to draw your own images. A child's drawing can make a really meaningful piece.

• Remember, part of the fun with this project is leaving the printed lines exposed. If you punch a color that only has one or two stitches in any given segment of the print, you can turn to the back side (in this case the loop side) and tie a square knot to secure it.

• You don't have to use the entire print. For the framed butterflies, I only selected 3 butterflies to emphasize from the print; the rest I simply punched over.

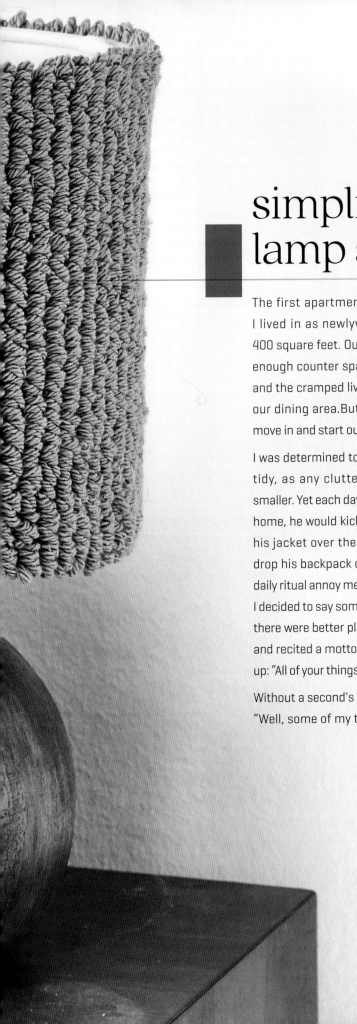

simplicity
lamp shade

The first apartment that Rauland and I lived in as newlyweds was less than 400 square feet. Our kitchen didn't have enough counter space for a microwave, and the cramped living room doubled as our dining area. But we couldn't wait to move in and start our lives together.

I was determined to keep the apartment tidy, as any clutter made it feel even smaller. Yet each day when Rauland came home, he would kick off his shoes, throw his jacket over the back of a chair, and drop his backpack on the table. I let this daily ritual annoy me for a few weeks, then I decided to say something. I told him that there were better places to put his things and recited a motto I was taught growing up: "All of your things should have a home."

Without a second's hesitation, he replied, "Well, some of my things are nomads." I

started laughing uncontrollably. I mean, who can argue with that kind of logic?

He did start paying more attention to how much space his things were taking up though, and together we began to declutter our home. At first, we were getting rid of things we knew we didn't need, and then we found ourselves being intentional about how we consumed and spent our time. What started as simplifying out of necessity became a way of life.

This lamp fits our style. It is simple, yet rich with color and texture. I chose not to include a pattern because sometimes keeping things as simple and clean as possible is exactly what a space needs. You can add a design if you'd like or use texture and color to add interest as I've done here.

MATERIALS:

Cylindrical lamp shade

Foundation cloth (enough to cover the
surface of the lamp shade)

Yarn, 1-3 skeins

Oxford Punch Needle, size 10 regular

Super glue

Scissors

Marker, permanent or water-based

Plastic or rubber gloves (optional)

Stretcher bar or gripper frame, 18"
(45.5 cm) or larger

Sewing machine

TECHNIQUES:

Ribbed Stitch (chapter 3)

Sewn Finish (chapter 4)

Glued Finish (chapter 4)

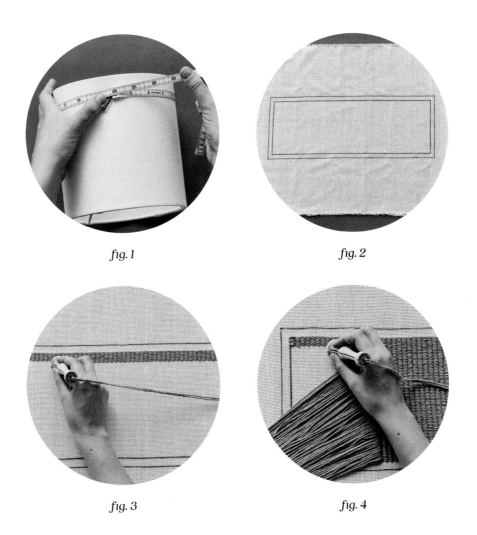

fig. 1

fig. 2

fig. 3

fig. 4

1. Measure the circumference and height of the lamp shade [**Figure 1**].

2. Outline the size measured onto the center of the foundation cloth, adding ⅛" (3 mm) to the length and height to account for yarn thickness. Mark a ½" (1.3 cm) seam allowance around all 4 sides [**Figure 2**].

3. Using a ribbed stitch, fill in the entire space that has been outlined, starting in a top corner, and stitching in horizontal rows [**Figure 3**]. If the lamp shade circumference is longer than the frame you are working with, hold the last stitch, and pull the yarn, leaving a tail 5 times longer than the length you have left to punch for the remainder of the lamp shade. Repeat this for every row.

4. Move the piece on the frame to finish the remainder [**Figure 4**]. Working one row at a time, thread each length of yarn from step 3 and finish punching each row.

NOTE: *You will need to thread the yarn from the opposite side of the needle than you normally would, because the punching is already mid-process in this step.*

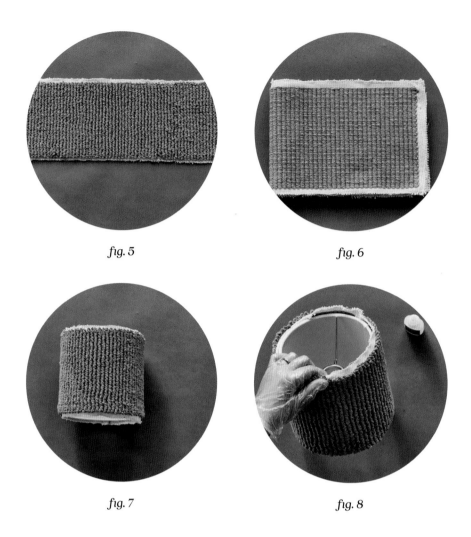

fig. 5

fig. 6

fig. 7

fig. 8

5. *Sew a zigzag around all 4 sides along the seam allowance marking, and cut away the excess fabric [**Figure 5**].*

6. With right sides together, fold the punched piece in half and sew down the side, creating a tube [**Figure 6**].

7. Turn right-side out and slip the punched tube over the lamp shade. It should be a snug fit [**Figure 7**].

8. Fold the excess fabric under, and glue in place along the top and bottom of the lamp shade [**Figure 8**].

Variations:
MIX IT UP

To add a pattern to your shade, you can:

• Use a ribbed stitch and a variegated yarn to create a fun and easy striped design.

• Use a ribbed stitch and several different colored yarns to punch bold, solid stripes.

• While the curved shape of the lamp shade pairs nicely with the ribbed stitch, don't feel limited to using just that stitch! You can use any stitch and patterning you like. My only advice: Don't use a flat stitch for this project as it creates bulkiness on the underside of the punched piece.

home zipper pouch

When I was eight years old, my family moved to a gorgeous little mountain town in Utah. I walked home from school each day with the breathtaking views of those majestic mountains. I drove through and around them, hiked their paths, and even watched in awe and despair as a wildfire stole life from them. Over the years, those mountains became the backdrop of my every day and eventually I stopped noticing them. I left for more than a decade, starting my own life and family. Then while writing this book, our family moved back to Utah and stayed with my parents while we looked for a place of our own. My daughters were now attending the same elementary school that I once did, and I found myself walking them home from school with those same mountains in the background. Once again, that stunning view became my norm, but this time I was determined not to take any of it for granted—the view or the amazing people who welcomed us home.

The design for this clutch is an abstracted mountain. I went through several renditions of this design, each time editing it down more and more. You might see a grid of dots shaping a triangle. But I see a collection of individuals, holding each other up. I see family, friends, and neighbors. Together, we are as majestic as the mountains I call "home."

MATERIALS

Monk's cloth, 24" (61 cm)

Cotton fabric for lining, (2) 10" (25.5 cm) squares

Leather-look vinyl, 10" × 4" (25.5 cm × 10 cm) rectangle

Leather-look vinyl, 10" (25.5 cm) square

Blue yarn, 1 skein

White yarn, 10 yards (9 m)

Matching thread

Oxford Punch Needle, size 10 regular

Hand sewing needle

Zipper, 9" (23 cm)

Scissors

Marker, permanent or water-based

Stretcher bars or gripper frame, 18" (45.5 cm)

Sewing machine

Zipper foot

TECHNIQUES

Basic Stitch (chapter 3)

Dotted Stitch (chapter 3)

Sewn Finish (chapter 4)

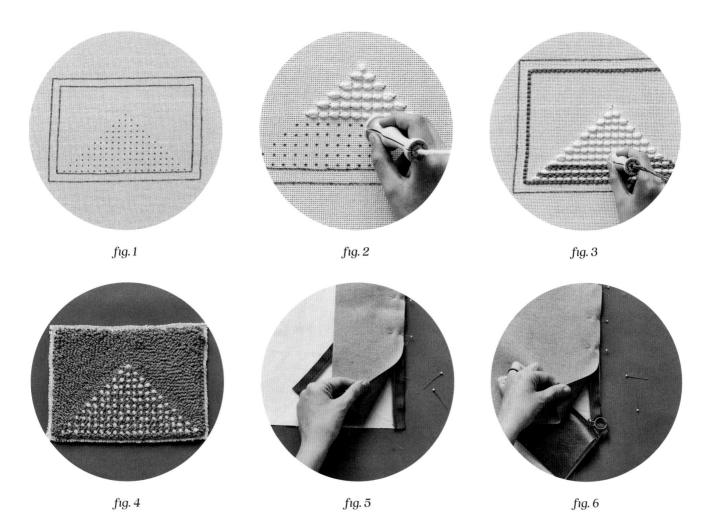

fig. 1

fig. 2

fig. 3

fig. 4

fig. 5

fig. 6

1. Draw a 6" × 9" (15 cm × 23 cm) rectangle, with a ½" (1.3 cm) seam allowance marked around the outer edge for sewing purposes. Mark each dot in the triangle, being sure to keep it centered (**Figure 1**). Secure the foundation cloth to the frame.

NOTE: *Rather than tracing these dots onto the monk's cloth, you can count squares for better accuracy (see Counting Squares in chapter 2). Each dot should be ⅜" (1 cm) apart. With my monk's cloth, this meant 1 dot for every 5 squares in the fabric. You will want to measure your own material to determine distance.*

2. Begin punching the white yarn using the dotted stitch. Punch into each marked dot (**Figure 2**).

3. Use a basic stitch to fill in the rest of the space (**Figure 3**).

4. Trim the excess fabric, leaving ½" (1.3 cm) seam allowance. Sew a zigzag around the edges (**Figure 4**).

5. With right sides together, pin the 10" × 4" (25.5. cm × 10 cm) leather-look vinyl rectangle to the outer edge of one side of the zipper. Pin the right side of the lining to the wrong side of the zipper in the same way. This should sandwich the zipper between the lining and the punched front of the pouch (**Figure 5**). Sew using a zipper foot.

6. Repeat step 5 with the remaining pieces of the leather-look vinyl and lining (**Figure 6**).

fig. 7

fig. 8

fig. 9

fig. 10

fig. 11

fig. 12

7. With right sides together, pin the bottom of the 10" × 4" (25.5 cm × 10 cm) leather-look vinyl rectangle to the top of the punched piece. Sew together using a ½" (1.3 cm) seam allowance (**Figure 7**).

8. With the pieces sewn to the zipper, sew around the sides and bottom of the pouch. To do this, align the lining pieces with right sides together, and the front and back of the pouch with right sides together. Pin (**Figure 8**). Leaving a 6" (15 cm) opening

at the bottom of the lining, sew around all sides using a ½" (1.3 cm) seam allowance.

9. Reinforce the corners with a few extra stitches, and trim corners a little bit, being careful not to clip the stitching. Turn pouch right-side out (**Figure 9**).

10. Tuck the raw edges of the lining under. Hand stitch the opening closed (**Figure 10**). Turn the lining into the pouch.

11. Press the lining and outer pouch pieces flat and top stitch around the upper edge of the pouch using a zipper foot (**Figure 11**).

12. Optional: embellish the zipper pull with a yarn tassel or leather pull (**Figure 12**) (see Making a Yarn Tassel on the next page).

Variations:

PERSONALIZED POUCH

The punch needle is simple enough for my daughters, ages seven and eight, to use. They love making zipper pouches as gifts for grandparents, friends, and teachers. Use the following directions to help a child make a custom zipper pouch using a hand drawn design, such as the pouches at left, which were designed by my own children.

1. Outline the size of the piece to be punched, in this case the measurements are 6" × 9" [15 cm × 23 cm].

2. Allow the child to draw their own design onto the foundation cloth. Children are frequently more comfortable with freeform drawing than adults, so they shouldn't need to trace anything. Just let them be creative!

3. If they are old enough to use a punch needle, allow them to punch the design themselves. If they are not ready to use a punch needle, have them select their own yarn colors, and then punch it for them, being sure to follow every adorable, imperfect line in their drawing.

4. Follow steps 4-12 in the Home Zipper Pouch to finish the zipper pouch.

fig. 1

fig. 2

Making a Yarn Tassel

1. Fold yarn repeatedly, so it is twice the length of the desired tassel (**Figure 1**). Insert one side of this folded yarn through the zipper pull.

2. Tie a tight square knot at the top of the tassel (**Figure 2**). Trim tassel as needed.

line animals
hoop art

When it comes to pen and paper, I'm a stick figure artist. I can't draw anything that's recognizable. So when my daughter asked me to make her a panda pillow for her bed, I froze. I don't know how to draw a panda! How could I possibly design a throw pillow with a panda that I don't know how to draw?

At that point, I did what any sensible (or insecure) artist would do—turn to the internet. I found image after image reaffirming my insecurity about my own artistic limits. Until, by the timely miscalculation of the search engine algorithm, my search accidentally brought up a photo of a panda origami. Its clean lines and abstract simplicity spoke to me. I turned to my notepad and sketched a geometric bear. It was almost what I wanted. But

not quite. And then it hit me. If I extended each line in my drawing to reach the outer edges of the page, it created this beautiful stained glass effect.

The pillow turned out awesome, if I do say so myself, and my supportive friends on Instagram seemed to agree. So I continued to try my hand at these long-lined animals. They have quickly become my favorite collection of work.

MATERIALS

Loosely woven fabric, 16" (40.5 cm) square

Black cotton string, 1 ball or skein

Variety of yarns, remnants

Oxford Punch Needle, size 10 regular

Scissors

Marker, water-based

Hoop frame, 12" (30.5 cm)

TECHNIQUES:

Flat Stitch (chapter 3)

Outline Stitch (chapter 3)

Hoop Frame (chapter 2)

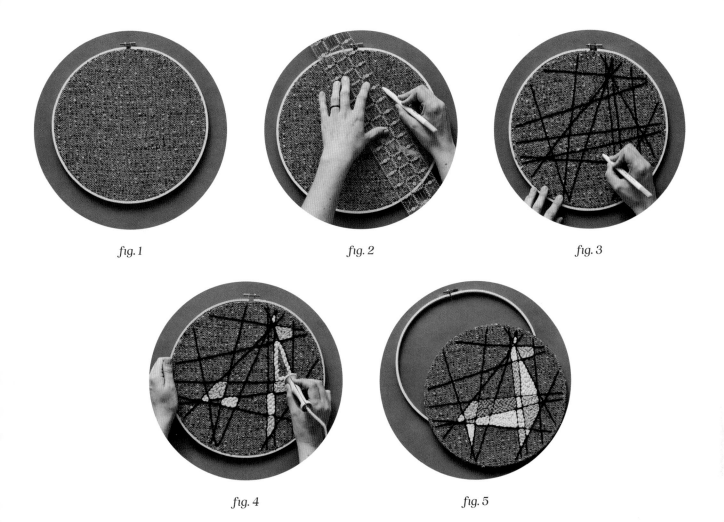

fig. 1　　　　　　　*fig. 2*　　　　　　　*fig. 3*

fig. 4　　　　　　　*fig. 5*

1. Using a loosely woven piece of fabric (mine was wool herringbone), prepare the hoop using the Hoop Frame method in chapter 2 (**Figure 1**).

2. Print a pattern for the animal of your choice. Trace the design onto your fabric, using the Window Transferring method found in chapter 2, or by using a ruler and your best general approximation of line placement (**Figure 2**).

NOTE: *Be sure to use a water-based marker for this project as the entire foundation cloth will not be filled in to cover any mistakes that are made with the marker.*

3. Use an outline stitch to trace all of the long lines in the pattern with black cotton string. Then mark the shapes that will be filled in so you don't lose sight of the animal as you work (**Figure 3**).

NOTE: *This is easier to do with a lightweight, light-colored material.*

4. Using a variety of yarns, fill in the animal, one shape at a time (**Figure 4**).

NOTE: *When using a decorative fabric, you can leave the outer shapes empty, since you've used a water-based marker, but if using monk's cloth or burlap, you may choose to fill in the outer shapes with a contrasting color scheme.*

5. Choose whether you would like to hang the piece with or without the outer embroidery hoop (**Figure 5**).

NOTE: *Traditionally, you wouldn't want to leave parts of your piece unpunched because it would have less strength and would be more likely to come loose. But the fact that this is a decorative wall hanging that will get no wear and tear will keep it from coming undone!*

Variations:

MAKE A MENAGERIE

To create your own animal design:

1. Decide which animal you want to punch.

2. Draw a rough sketch of the animal. Remember, your sketch doesn't have to be pretty; that's how the whole concept for this project came to be.

3. Use a ruler and pencil to draw distinctive lines that run across the entire length of the page. Start with aspects like the top of the head, the ears, the back, the legs, etc.

4. As you draw these lines, make small markings along the way to help you keep track of where the animal is hiding within the lines. This can be tricky!

5. If you make a mistake, don't worry! Just trace the lines you do like onto a new piece of paper and keep trying.

6. Once you are pleased with the design and each small shape making up the animal is marked, transfer your design to the foundation cloth of your choice and start punching.

life pillow

Growing up, I lived for summer days reserved for nothing but scissors and glue. And maybe some funky ribbon.

I remember being in the car with my family and telling my parents all about the things I wanted to make. I was getting more and more animated as the list went on until finally, exasperated, I exclaimed, "I just have too many ideas and not enough time to do them!"

Moments later, we turned a corner and saw a man sitting in a lawn chair in his front yard, watching the cars drive by. My dad pointed to the man and said with a smirk, "That guy needs some of your ideas!"

As a mother, I can see this same enthusiasm in my kids. They will spend hours digging through the recycling and building imaginative worlds filled with imagination. Our kitchen table is permanently scarred with glitter glue, and their play space is almost always littered with scraps of paper and crayons. Eat, sleep, craft, repeat.

This particular pillow boasts a bold, repeating geometric design. I love working with repetition. It allows you to scale a project up or down to your liking and creates a simple yet intriguing busyness. It's much like life: Repetitive, yet somehow exciting all the same.

MATERIALS:

Monk's cloth, 24" (61 cm)

Pillow back fabric, 2 pieces 18" × 16"
(45.5 cm × 40.5 cm)

White yarn, 1 skein

Black yarn, 3 skeins

Matching thread

Oxford Punch Needle, size 10 regular

Pillow insert, 18" (45.5 cm)

Scissors

Marker, permanent or water-based

Stretcher bars or gripper frame,
20" (51 cm)

Sewing machine

TECHNIQUES:

Basic Stitch (chapter 3)

Flat Stitch (chapter 3)

Sewn Finish (chapter 4)

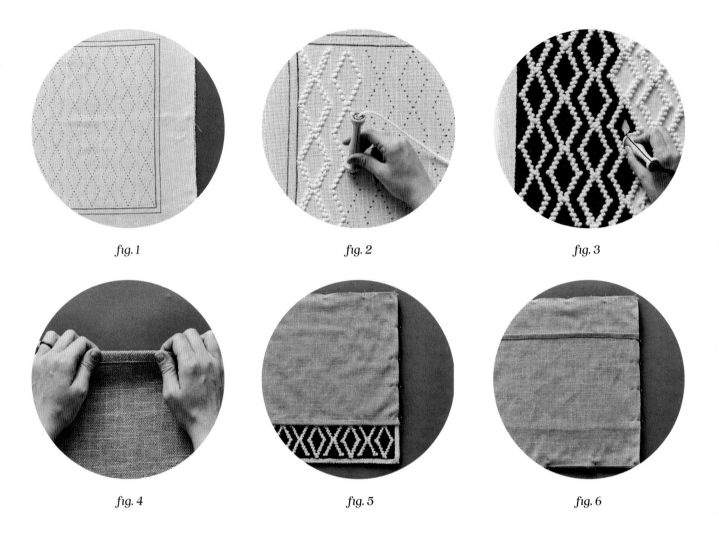

fig. 1   *fig. 2*   *fig. 3*

fig. 4   *fig. 5*   *fig. 6*

1. Draw an 18" (46 cm) outline onto the monk's cloth. Add ½" (1.3 cm) seam allowance to all sides for sewing purposes later. Draw in the geometric pattern. This is best done by counting squares (up four, over two) to create the rows of diamonds (**Figure 1**).

2. Secure foundation cloth to frame and use a basic stitch to trace the diamond pattern with white yarn. I chose to go over the pattern twice with the white to make it as bold as possible (**Figure 2**).

3. Use a flat stitch to fill in the rest of the pattern with black yarn (**Figure 3**). Trim the excess fabric leaving ½" (1.3 cm) seam allowance. Sew a zigzag around the edges.

4. Fold down one long side of a pillow back piece ½" (1.3 cm), and then another ½" (1.3 cm) to create a double hem. Pin and top stitch. Repeat on the other pillow back piece (**Figure 4**).

5. With right sides together, align one pillow back piece with the top of the pillow and the hemmed edge of the pillow back toward the center of the pillow as shown; pin in place (**Figure 5**).

6. Align the second pillow back piece at the bottom of the pillow, with the hemmed edge of the pillow back toward the center of the pillow as shown; pin (**Figure 6**).

7. Sew along all four sides [**Figure 7**].

8. Turn the pillow cover right-side out [**Figure 8**]. Fill with the pillow insert.

fig. 7

fig. 8

Variations:
A PLETHORA OF PILLOWS

Make a pillow with any shape, colors, or pattern. Here's how:

1. Determine the size you want the finished pillow to be. Mark the outline of the pillow dimensions onto the foundation cloth, leaving room for a seam allowance.

2. Punch the design. It could be a nature-inspired image, a repetitive pattern, or even something as simple as a stripe.

3. Cut two pieces of fabric for the pillow backing: Each should be the same width as the pillow front (with a seam allowance) and about ¾ the length of the pillow front.

4. Sew the pillow together as instructed in steps 4–8 in the Life Pillow project.

inward tapestry

In our ten years of marriage, Rauland and I have moved fourteen times, experiencing rural, suburban, and city living along the way. In all the places we have lived, we have never had a formal entryway. Every front door opened into the heart of our home.

There were times when this lack of privacy bothered me, but over the years I came to appreciate and even prefer it. There is no barrier to shield our guests from the mess of our everyday lives. When a visitor stops by unannounced, they will see dishes on the counter, and toys strewn about the house. For a long time I found myself apologizing for these messes, but I've since come to embrace it. Our home is lived in and a welcome place for anyone who wants to enter.

I recently had an idea for a triangular shaped rug, which I envisioned at the front door, pointing our guests inward. At the time, we were house hunting, and I had no idea if a rug of that shape or size would fit in a home we hadn't even found yet. But I made it anyway.

A few months later, we moved into our current home and I was delighted to discover that my triangular rug fit perfectly at our front door. And there it sits, day after day, pointing our guests inward.

This tapestry is a smaller version of my triangular rug. It's a more manageable size for a beginner to make but can certainly be scaled to the size of a full rug.

MATERIALS

Monk's cloth, 22" (56 cm)

Fabric strips, 8 yards (7.3 m)

Purple yarn, 1 skein

Beige yarn, 1 skein

Cotton string, 5 yds (4.6 m)

Oxford Punch Needle, size 10 regular

Stretcher bars or gripper frame, 18" (45.5 cm)

Tapestry needle

Wooden dowel, 26" (66 cm)

Scissors

Marker, permanent or water-based

TECHNIQUES

Basic Stitch (chapter 3)

Flat Stitch (chapter 3)

Ribbed Stitch (chapter 3)

Heightened Stitch (chapter 3)

Fringe Finish (chapter 4)

Whipped Edge Finish (chapter 4)

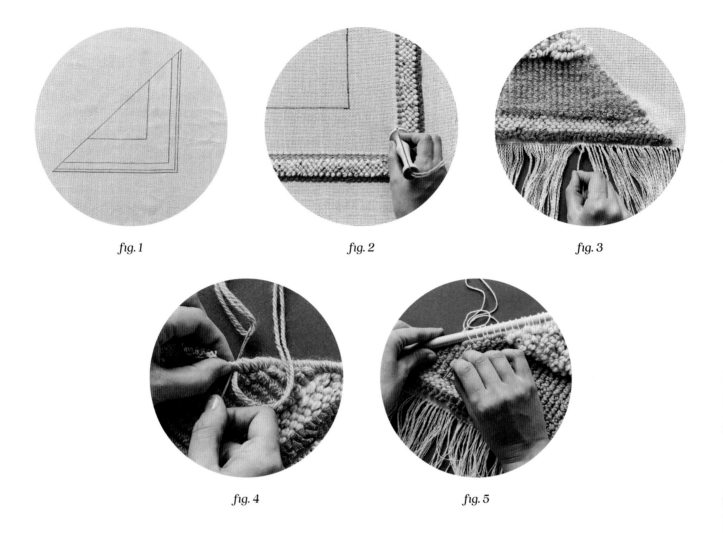

fig. 1

fig. 2

fig. 3

fig. 4

fig. 5

1. Outline the tapestry design on the monk's cloth, with two 15" [38 cm] sides forming a right angle. Connect the two lines to create the third side of the triangle. Draw an angled stripe into the design as shown (**Figure 1**).

2. Secure the foundation cloth to the frame and begin punching each stripe with different yarns and stitches (**Figure 2**):

Row 1: Basic stitch with fabric strips

Row 2: Flat stitch with beige yarn

Row 3: Ribbed stitch with mauve yarn

Row 4: Heightened stitch with beige yarn

3. Finish the two 15" [38 cm] sides of the tapestry with fringe following the instructions in chapter 4 (**Figure 3**). Trim the length of the fringe to 3" [7.5 cm].

4. Trim the excess fabric along the top, leaving 1" [2.5 cm] for binding. Be careful not to cut any fringe. Sew a zigzag along entire length. Use the whipped-edge binding method found in chapter 4 to finish the long side of the tapestry (**Figure 4**).

5. Use a tapestry needle and cotton string to attach the tapestry to the wooden dowel as shown (**Figure 5**).

scrappy rug

I've always loved the challenge of making the most out of what seems like nothing, especially when it comes to scraps. As a teenager, I once upcycled a pair of knit bell-bottoms—mustard yellow with a white pin stripe—into a swimsuit. It was unbelievably scratchy but adorable, so obviously I wore it anyway. I just couldn't help but reuse materials that might otherwise get thrown out.

I'm still this way with remnants. I can't bear to let any go to waste. There is always potential for forgotten scraps to become something spectacular. That's where this rug comes in. As the last project in *Punched*, I found it fitting to create a simple design that could utilize yarn remnants from previous projects. The way I see it, a rug like this tells more than one story—it tells the tale of every other piece of art that came from those same materials.

Of course, if you don't happen to have yarn scraps on hand, a variegated yarn would work wonderfully for a similar effect!

MATERIALS

Monk's cloth, 48" × 36" (122 cm × 91.5 cm)

Navy rug yarn, 6 skeins

Remnants or variegated yarn, 6 skeins

Oxford Punch Needle, size 10 regular

Scissors

Marker, permanent or water-based

Stretcher bars or gripper frame, any size

TECHNIQUES

Basic Stitch (chapter 3)

Whipped Edge Finish (chapter 4)

Fringe Finish (chapter 4)

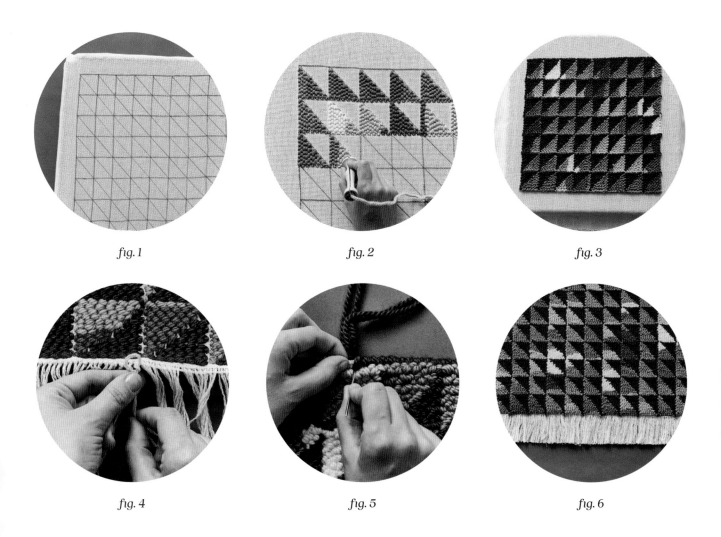

fig. 1

fig. 2

fig. 3

fig. 4

fig. 5

fig. 6

1. Mark a 24" × 36" (61 cm × 91.5 cm) outline on the backing cloth, then draw a triangular pattern, with 2" (5 cm) right triangles (**Figure 1**).

2. Secure the foundation cloth to the frame and use a basic stitch to fill in every other triangle covering the entire rug with remnant yarns or variegated yarn, being especially careful not to stitch too tightly (**Figure 2**).

3. Continue using a basic stitch to fill in the rest of the rug with navy blue yarn, moving the rug on the frame as needed (**Figure 3**).

4. Following the directions in chapter 4, add fringe to the (2) 24" (61 cm) sides of the rug (**Figure 4**).

5. Following the directions in chapter 4 and using the navy blue yarn, bind the last two sides of the rug with a whipped edge finish (**Figure 5**).

6. Using a damp cloth and a warm iron, press the rug flat, focusing on the outer edges of the rug to prevent it from curling under (**Figure 6**).

FREQUENTLY ASKED QUESTIONS

The following are some of the most frequent questions that I get asked. Hopefully, these troubleshooting tips will make your needle punching a success.

My stitches won't stay in place. What's wrong?

There are a few reasons why stitches come loose (**Figure 1**):

• The yarn is too heavy for the punch needle. If the yarn can't glide smoothly, it won't move through the needle as quickly as you are trying to punch. Try holding the previous stitch in place with an index finger while punching your next stitch. If that doesn't work, the yarn may be too thick for the tool (**Figure 2**).

• The yarn is too light for the punch needle. If the strand of yarn is too thin, there won't be enough tension to keep it in place. Try doubling or even tripling the yarn when threading the needle (**Figure 3**).

• Your stitches are too long. When using a punch needle, you are typically supposed to move the tip about ¼" (6 mm) between stitches. If your stitches are longer, the loops may pop out of place. Some of the stitches in chapter 3 bend this rule a bit, and as such, try using an index finger to hold the previous stitch in place while punching your next stitch (**Figure 2**).

• Your foundation cloth isn't tight enough on the frame. If there is a lot of give in the foundation cloth when you're punching, the needle can't function properly. In this case, take the foundation cloth off the frame and set it up again (**Figure 4**).

How do I fix loose stitches?

Sometimes a stitch will come loose while you are working on a project, and occasionally (although it's not common) a stitch will come loose after a project is complete (**Figure 5**). There are two simple ways to fix the problem:

• Pull the yarn back to the location of the missed stitch and start again (**Figure 6**).

• From the right side of the project, use a standard rug hook or crochet hook to pull the loop back up to the surface (**Figure 7**).

How much yarn will I need?

There are two ways to determine this:

• Using a size 10 regular Oxford Punch Needle with a basic stitch will give you about 10" (25.4 cm) square of punched surface for every skein of medium-weight yarn. This type of estimate obviously requires some guesswork, as there are

variables in the yarn and punch needle used. But this is a good way to calculate how much yarn to get before you begin or how much to get if you need more.

• Punch a 1" (2.5 cm) square using the same materials and techniques you plan to use for your project. Pull the yarn out (see Frogging in chapter 3). Measure the length from that 1" (2.5 cm) square (**Figure 8**) and use it to calculate yarn usage on a larger scale for your project. Buy a bit more yarn than you need to account for wastage and stitching inconsistencies.

What if I'm part way through and don't like the colors or design?

Frogging offers an easy solution. Just pull on the yarn from the flat side and lift it out (**Figure 9**). Save the yarn for another project, and re-punch on the same foundation cloth. See Making Mistakes in chapter 3 for tips.

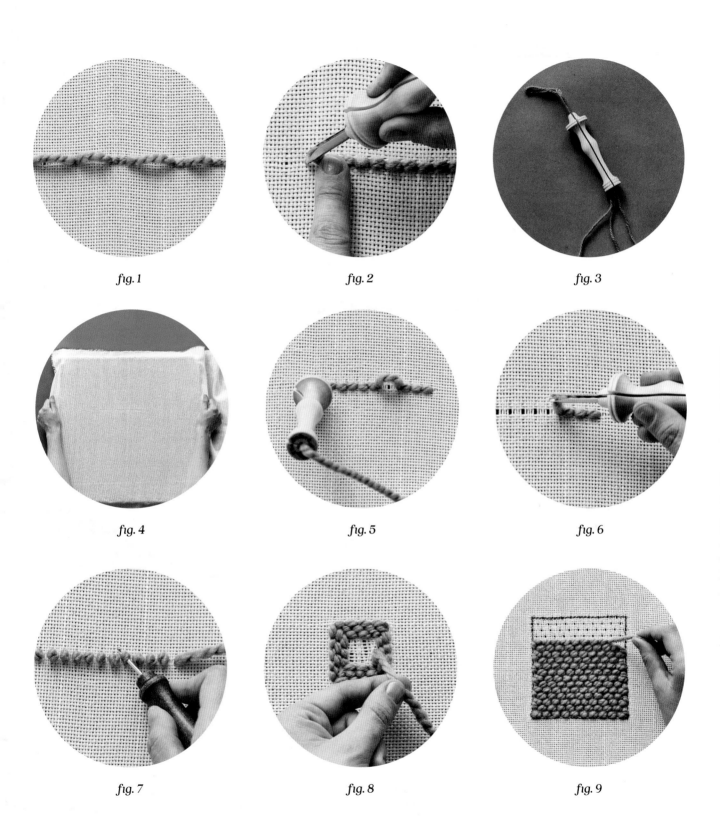

fig. 1

fig. 2

fig. 3

fig. 4

fig. 5

fig. 6

fig. 7

fig. 8

fig. 9

How do I know if I'm using the right yarn?

There are no hard and fast rules. If the yarn glides easily through the punch needle, you can use it. And different yarn types create different textures. Bring your punch needle when yarn shopping. It will help you determine if the yarn will work in the tool. Think about durability and washability when choosing yarn for any project.

What type of yarn do you prefer to work with?

I'm most drawn to cotton and wool because natural materials age well and are beautiful to work with.

I took my project off the frame and the edges are curling in. What can I do?

Even when you are careful not to use tight stitches, the edges may curl due to the density of the loop side of the project relative to the flat side (**Figure 10**). Iron the edges flat using a damp press cloth and the proper heat setting for the type of yarn fibers being used (**Figure 11**).

How do I wash my punched piece?

Punched rugs are machine washable! Before washing anything, make sure all of the edges are finished (bound, fringed, or sewn; see chapter 4) to prevent the foundation cloth from fraying in the wash. Wash on a delicate cycle and hang dry.

How long does it take to learn to use a punch needle?

Using a punch needle is actually quite intuitive. In fact, my daughters (ages 7 and 8) love to punch and can do so with little help. Usually one sitting is enough to start getting comfortable using a punch needle. Of course, certain projects require more time and patience than others, so it depends on what you plan to make.

What do I do with the yarn tails as I work?

Pull them through to the loop side, and trim the yarn tails the same height as the loops when you're completely finished punching (**Figure 12**). See changing colors in chapter 2 for tips.

If you don't tie any knots or use glue, how does it keep from coming undone?

The stitches and loops are packed in tightly, so everything holds in place nicely. The flat side does have the potential to snag, but the loop side, which is usually displayed as the front, is very strong. You'll find punched rugs are surprisingly durable.

Do you glue the back of rugs?

Some rug hookers do, but I prefer not to. The back doesn't need to be glued to be strong. Also, if you do glue it and the rug gets a snag, you can't fix it. If it isn't glued, you can easily fix the snag.

What is your favorite source for tools and materials?

Unfortunately, punch needle supplies aren't always readily available at craft stores. I expect that to change as the craft increases in popularity. In the meantime, it's quite easy to find what you need online. See chapter 1 for more information about my favorite tools and materials. You should be able to find standard embroidery hoops, stretcher bar frames, burlap, and yarn at your local craft store.

fig. 10

fig. 11

fig. 12

about the author

Stacie Schaat is the artist and founder of Yellow Spool. She is a mother of three, stealing quiet moments to create wherever she can. Her background in education and textile art have fueled her love of making, and teaching others to embrace their own creativity.

www.yellowspool.com

@yellowspool

dedication

To Rauland, my favorite person, without whom I may never have discovered my love of rug hooking.

acknowledgments

A special thank you:

To Rose Pearlman, a fellow punch needle artist and friend, who opened the door for this book to become a reality for me.

To Kerry Bogert, who encouraged me when I felt inadequate, and pushed me to a better place, beyond my comfort zone.

To Jodi Butler, who believed in me, and patiently helped me edit my ideas, from conception to completion.

To the entire F+W Media / Interweave team, who carefully took my vision for this book, and made it into something more beautiful than I could have ever imagined.

To Amy Oxford, for providing my favorite Oxford Company tools and supplies for the making of this book.

To Seal Harbor Rug Co., for supplying me with my favorite rug yarn, used throughout the book.

To my parents, who have cheered me on through every creative endeavor I've attempted since childhood.

And most importantly, to my husband and children—my biggest supporters, and the reason behind everything that I create.

index

what are you making next?

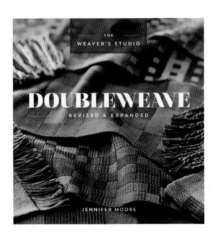

Doubleweave
Revised & Expanded

JENNIFER MOORE

9781632506443

$29.99

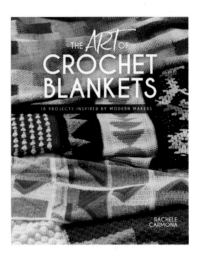

The Art of Crochet Blankets

18 Projects Inspired by Modern Makers

RACHELE CARMONA

9781632505736

$24.99

Tula Pink Coloring with Thread

Stitching a Whimsical World with Hand Embroidery

TULA PINK

9781440248115

$21.99

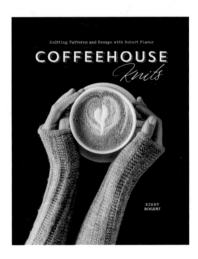

Coffeehouse Knits

Knitting Patterns and Essays with Robust Flavor

KERRY BOGERT

9781632506597

$26.99

 Interweave